INVISIBLE LAW OF
THE UNIVERSE

INVISIBLE LAW OF THE UNIVERSE

The Beauty of Harmony

KAY FORGIONE

This book is dedicated to…
God
and
humanity

CONTENTS

INTRODUCTION

HARMONIC LAW IS MATHEMATICAL, UNIVERSAL, AND TRANSCENDENTAL LAW

Harmonic law, identified with the mathematical symbol Φ, can be detected in every beauty of nature on Earth. Its omnipresence is not confined just to nature around us. Its omnipresence in the universe also applies to the motion of human society to gauge the degree of aesthetic quality mirroring the same law. The scope of this treatise—my focus—is solely human society and its ideal formation to ensure happiness of all in it.

I believe that cosmic harmony, created by the supreme intellectual being (Prime Mover or God or whatever you may call it), offers a powerful message through harmonic law, producing splendid grandeur, similar to musical chords that please our internal sensibility, although we cannot explain the nature of it with human words. It can be poetic, philosophical, or mathematical. But in any case, it must, in my view, have something to do with our soul that is communicated by the Cosmic Master to grasp the beauty of harmony. The grandeur of cosmic arrangement is beyond our possibility of calculation or reasoning. But the sublimity can be felt in our soul when it is moved by divine will of God who is the most sublime in every way. The cosmic sphere is not a static existence as we know it; rather, it is an eternally evolving energy of beauty that constantly refines our soul and thoughts. Of course, this is a metaphysical concept. But the means of expression, as far as we are concerned, is our rational capability. Simply put, human rationality can produce a harmonic melody of the universe. I believe it is precisely this paramount coexistence of metaphysical conception of God and human rationality that brings a hope of making our Earth planet more livable and sustainable as part of the larger universe, articulating the beauty of harmony. It is with our rationality that we can practice harmony with our actions, just as skilled musicians do, by grasping the intention and principles of the composer who creates a beautiful consonance. I am thoroughly convinced, through modern scientific information, that corporeality is nothing but a reflection of invisible reality. This conviction has not resulted from a simple religious faith but from modern scientific knowledge abundantly available for us today. Regretfully the religious canons and ideas of virtue influenced human society in the past are slowly disappearing from modern society with the overpowering influence of science that deals with fragmentary analyses most of the time. Consequently, our rationality is missing out on the large picture: an invisible reality of grandeur formed in cosmic harmony that we are a part of. (Human rationality is expounded in chapter 2.)

PRINCIPLES OF HUMAN VIRTUE IN PURSUING HAPPINESS

Happiness—the goal of human life—is dependent on the degree of cultivation of virtue, the practice of goodness developed by the intellectual part of the soul. If we agree that happiness is the aim of the individual, then the government's aim is to ensure the happiness of every citizen of a nation by exercising civic virtue, reviving Aristotle's idea of human society. More specifically, in our modern society the role of government is of paramount importance for mitigating countless social maladies caused by economic inequality (discussed in chapters 10 and 11 of this book). A strong government, while encouraging capitalism that produces the supply side, is a necessity to redistribute the capital to the poor. In other words, the supply side of economy must be in harmony with the demand side to maintain social equilibrium so that human civilization can continue to prosper without disruption. For today's mass society, this balancing power undoubtedly is only in the hands of government.

Human virtue comprises not merely moral behavior but also the intellectual judgment necessary for joint survival in the face of the exponential growth of the human population and shrinking natural resources on the planet today. In this context, I would highlight humanism and compassion, emphasized by Christ and Buddha, as essential principles of human virtue that can build peaceful interdependence among people. This interdependence is quite different from past experiences of exploiter-exploited or controller-controlled relationships. It is rather helping one another through cooperation, without encroaching on each other's independent states of life.

IS CAPITALISM IN VIOLATION OF HARMONIC LAW?

Human survival has a long history in terms of the evolution of *Homo sapiens* although it is considered only a few brief seconds on the cosmic calendar.[1] It started as individual survival, fighting against tough surroundings, and then became tribal protection against intruders, which evolved gradually into nationhood in the modern concept of society for joint prosperity and civilization. A nation itself, in the sense of a political association, with a written constitution ordained by law and administered by elected officials, is widely practiced today upholding the principles of freedom and equal rights of individual citizens. Capitalism is thriving in such a free democratic society wherein a new type of oligarchy is growing portentously, dividing society between the mega-rich minority and the poor majority. Thus today's democracy seems to facilitate itself only as a means to reach the goal of capitalism while struggling to maintain the noble ideas of equality and liberty.

---

[1] The 13.7-billion-year lifetime of the universe mapped onto a single year. At this scale the big bang takes place on January 1 at midnight and each second is 434 years. The scale was popularized by Carl Sagan in his book *The Dragons of Eden*. Human, archeological, and historical times, tracing back to the beginning of the Bronze Age, are only at the last fifteen seconds or so of the cosmic calendar at midnight on December 31.

The fundamental conflict is in the distribution of capital—an imbalance between accumulation of wealth in the hands of capitalists and distribution of wealth to workers. Thus the tension between democracy and capitalism is growing steadily. It should be noted, however, that the impulse to acquisition per se (the pursuit to gain the greatest possible amount of money) has little to do with capitalism at its inception, for this type of impulse has been recognized as part of human nature throughout the history of mankind. Thus, unlimited greed for gain itself is not directly identified with capitalism. What would be the chief characteristics of capitalism then?

Capitalism is a system of economics based on private ownership of capital and production of goods or services for profit. That is to say, the ultimate goal of capitalism is identified with the pursuit of profit, hopefully perpetual profit, by means of continuous capitalistic enterprise. Where capitalistic acquisition is rationally pursued, the corresponding action is justified in terms of profit added to capital. This means that the action is adapted to a systematic mobilization of capital, goods, or services as a means of acquisition so that the ending balance of monetary assets exceeds the initial capital at the end of the business cycle. Everything is measured by financial balances: an initial balance before any probable profitability and the ending balance in terms of how much profit has been made. Simply put, the important fact is always profit. This is how modern corporations operate in capitalistic society. The word "corporation" derives from corpus, the Latin word for body or a body of people. Thus, a corporation is owned and controlled by its members. The day-to-day activities of a corporation are typically controlled by individuals appointed by board members. In this way, the corporation will survive in perpetuity—longer than the lives of any individual members. It may continue forever, irrespective of the longevity of its directors, except in the case where the corporation is dissolved or liquidated.

Along with such a corporate structure, now the peculiar modern Western form of capitalism has been expanded in an accelerated fashion by the development of scientific technologies. Its rationality is thus essentially dependent on the most important technical factors that assure the expected profitability. Today, sure enough, we see technology beginning to take its place as a primary driver of profitability and market competition in every industry. We see that large and often long-established companies have started using technology as a way of not only improving their own internal processes but also using it as driving force to grow rapidly and expand as the next logical step. Thus, the development of these sciences and the technologies resting upon them now receives important stimulation from these capitalistic interests. This of course is farther away from the origin of Western science, which did not involve such interests. But the technical utilization of scientific knowledge—so important for the living conditions of the masses—soon became a major economic consideration, alongside the development of economic rationalism. The economic rationality of course did not miss out on the consumers' demand. As the rising demand for devices becomes more interconnected with their daily life, the consumers continue to demonstrate their demand for more convenient devices. Thus it became inevitable for large businesses in capitalistic societies to employ technology for the purpose of profitmaking. Undoubtedly the crux of rational decision and conduct implicate mass production, thereby expecting mass consumption. Due to the ability and ingenuity of humans adopting certain types of practical rational conduct, this sort of rationalism seems to fit the bill in the scheme of national politics. It revolves around the question of how to make a country richer and powerful. Therefore, national politics took capitalism as its bedfellow, not realizing that this seemingly innocent bedfellow would grow monstrously large and powerful to influence national ethics and morality, not to mention the destiny of the nation.

As we witness, the capitalist economic system with little government intervention seems to produce so much misery for the vast majority of the population in the whirlwind of increased material wealth. We can see that capitalism does not make all of us happier, wiser, kinder, and more spiritually enlightened. It does not mean we should get rid of private property, but we do need a more thoughtful, prudent relationship between wealth and its distribution for the happiness of all. Therefore, it's about time we begin seriously to consider reforming capitalism, not by simply condemning the mega wealth of giant corporations but by revising the rationalistic contents of economic behaviors of both the governing and governed. Only then will we truly be able to imagine an economy that not only is productive and innovative but also fosters human freedom and fulfillment.

WE HAVE WILLPOWER TO DO SOMETHING GOOD FOR ALL

The central theme of this book is about human happiness and universal harmony. When the universal harmony is destroyed by excess capitalism, the social discordance is unavoidable. The discourse throughout this book, therefore, consists of detailed investigations of various aspects of capitalism in America that represents the epitome of capitalism in the world today and of contemporary social mores that have been introduced and shaped by capitalism. Ultimately in this discussion, I attempted, in full support of the Organization for European Economic Co-operation and Development (OECD), to explore the possibility of building a society that not only brings greater prosperity and happiness for all citizens but also a better relationship to nature, to one another, and to ourselves. In this context, I would like to draw the reader's attention to the intellectual voice of the OECD urging each and every national government to practice civic virtue to nurture human happiness and joint survival.

Undoubtedly human societies must obey the same harmonic law established for cosmic harmony to survive and thrive on Earth. Undeniably, virtuous souls can, in a profound way, comprehend cosmic harmony through universal wisdom. An expansion of such wisdom among political elites is paramount for unanimous consensus on the imminent issue of the increasing gap of inequality between the rich and poor. In the midst of the breathtaking speed of technological evolution, the concentration of wealth in the hands of a minority, along with the apathetic attitude of the governments of rich nations, such as the United States, that leave the poor masses with a small piece of the pie, is foreshadowing an inevitable doom.

Chapter 1

HARMONIC LAW

MATHEMATICAL TRUTH

The word "mathematics" comes from the ancient Greek language and means "what one gets to know" or "study"; in modern Greek it just means "lesson." In the present day, the comprehensive definition of mathematics probably would be the study of numbers, equations, functions, and geometric shapes and their relationships. Some of its major subdivisions are arithmetic, algebra, geometry, and calculus. Undoubtedly, modern science and technology could not have developed without a mathematical foundation, and at the same time it has been the solid vehicle connecting human intellect to the study of the universe.

The universe is full of numbers that can be arranged to reveal certain cosmic truths. Galileo Galilei (1564–1642) said, "The universe cannot be read until we have learned the language and become familiar with the characters in which it is written. It is written in mathematical language, and the letters are triangles, circles and other geometrical figures, without which means it is humanly impossible to comprehend a single word. Without these, one is wandering about in a dark labyrinth."[2] In our endeavor to understand the structure or the principles that underlie the organization of the cosmos mathematically,

---

2 Galileo Galilei, *Il Saggiatore* (*The Assayer*), translated by Stillman Drake in his book *Discoveries and Opinions of Galileo* pp. 237-8 (Doubleday & Company, 1957)

we need to perceive that harmony is the primal cosmic law, engendering not only procreation and propagation but also producing the exquisite beauty in all things. Pythagoras (570–495 BC) recognized a strong connection between mathematics and beauty, noticing particularly that objects proportioned by the golden ratio (ϕ) were the most beautiful.

Johannes Kepler (1571–1630), a major revolutionary of seventeenth-century science in Europe, is best known for his laws of planetary motion, based on his works *Astronomia nova, Harmonices Mundi*, and *Epitome Astronomiae Copernicanae*. These works provided one of the foundations for Isaac Newton's theory of universal gravitation. In *Harmonices Mundi (The Harmony of the World)*, published in 1619, Kepler discusses the law of planetary motion as "music of the spheres," while seeking to understand a rational arrangement of the cosmic bodies.

When Kepler used the term "harmony," he did not strictly refer to the musical definition but rather a broader definition encompassing congruence in nature and the workings of both the celestial and terrestrial bodies. He established celestial-harmonic relationships by geometrical calculation of musical ratios, and these relationships convinced him that God is acting as a grand geometer who created harmonic law for the universe. Kepler believed that the chief aim of all investigations of the external world should be to discover the rational order and harmony that have been preordained by God, revealed to us in the language of mathematics.

IMPLICATION OF π

Contemplating cosmic harmony and its elegant beauty, we perhaps can think that God's primal design of the universe lies in two very fundamental cosmic principles displayed in mathematics. These are the geometric circle powered by pi (π) and the Pythagorean right triangle powered by phi (ϕ). The pi clearly plants deep pondering in our intellect, awakening the awareness of cosmic splendor and its beauty. The circle describes infinity, yet it is the sign of cosmic unity—unity of visible and invisible—embraced by infinite power and love,. Thus, π is the sign of the cosmic reality of God's grace, emanating from the center.

Believing that nothing exists without a center, mathematical philosophers started with a point and drew a circle around it. This symbol is called the *monad* and represents the number one, or atom 1. This center is the most stable essence as the foundation to bring the circle into unity. No wonder Pythagoras called the monad "God and the good." The monad is the seed of a tree, for which numbers are to the monad as branches of a tree are to the seed. The monad in relation to other numbers preserves the identity of every other number or anything it encounters. Any number multiplied by one is itself, and any number divided by one is itself.

Pythagoreans believed that nothing exists without a center, around which it revolves. The center is the source, and it is beyond understanding—it is unknowable. But like a seed, the center will expand and will fulfill itself as a circle. Through modern scientific proof, we now know that galaxies orbit a single central point, and the same law applies to even the atomic level—the basic building block of all matter. Pi seems to me the symbol of divine energy flowing out of this cosmic center.

The calculation of π reached five trillion digits today, and the digits keep growing with no ending. Thus, it is called a transcendental number, as German mathematician and philosopher Gottfried Wilhelm Leibniz (1646–1716) coined it.[3] The term "transcendental" simply means that its existence is beyond our experience and knowledge. Leonhard Euler (1707–83) later used the symbol of π, stating that "for the sake of brevity we will write this number as "π"[4] and the practice was universally adopted thereafter. As one can imagine, modern scientific equations are loaded with this transcendental number; even its decimal fraction expansions go on forever and never repeat at any stage.

---

3 Leibniz coined the term "transcendental" in his 1682 paper in which he proved that the sine function is not an algebraic function. Source: *Historical Dictionary of Leibniz's Philosophy* (Scarecrow Press, 2006).

4 The earliest known use of the Greek letter π to represent the ratio of a circle's circumference to its diameter was by Welsh mathematician William Jones in his 1706 *work Synopsis Palmariorum Matheseos or A New Introduction to the Mathematics*. After Jones introduced the Greek letter in 1706, it was not adopted by other mathematicians until Euler started using it, beginning with his 1736 work *Mechanica*.

Some scientists suspect that our universe, as we know it now, doesn't have any purpose. To them, perhaps, the universe is just a composition of material, space, and time. But such a conclusion leaves many nagging questions unanswered: Why does the universe exist? Was it created by someone or something? To put it another way, is there a hidden law to the parameters ruling the cosmic world? Such questions compel human intellect with a resolute quest to understand the eternal grandeur of the universe. When you are drawn toward the quest for universal truth, and as long as the quest for truth persists, not only can you trust your intellect, but you can also trust the universe, which expands in such an exquisite and timeless way, opening itself to myriad splendors that are truly sublime. That's the spirit of the Universal Master, we call God. The sublime is eternal beauty—the quality of grandeur. Such grandeur is beyond all possibility of calculation or reasoning. Sublimity can be felt in our soul when it is mobilized by a divine tensor of the Master, who is the most sublime in every way. The cosmic sphere is not a static existence as we know it; rather, it is an eternally evolving energy of beauty that constantly refines our soul and thoughts. Immanuel Kant (1724–1804), in 1764, recorded his thoughts on the feeling of the beautiful and sublime. To him, the sublime is boundless and formless but has dynamic and mathematical energy.

There is no doubt that mathematics is the best vehicle for reaching out for universal splendors with rigorous deduction from appropriately chosen axioms and definitions. It seems to me that every piece of truth discovered through mathematics imparts a very profound message for us to ponder the Master's thinking. According to Srinivasa Ramanujan (1887–1920), an equation is meaningless to him unless it expresses a thought of God. He often said that in mathematics alone, one can have a concrete realization of God.[5] Ramanujan was an Indian mathematician and autodidact who, with almost no formal training in pure mathematics, made extraordinary contributions to mathematical analysis, number theory, series, and continued fractions. Rumanujan's talent has been compared to legendary mathematicians such as Euler, Gauss, Newton, and Archimedes.

---

5 *The Man Who Knew Infinity,* Robert Kanigel (Washington Square Press, 1991)

Cosmologically speaking, as contemporary scientists suspect, an un-known number of universes are in existence beyond the galaxy universe in which our solar system resides. The multiverse concept is derived from the idea of eternal expansion, in which the inflationary period our universe start-ed right after the big bang.

If we set aside cosmology for a moment, the circle manifests symboli-cally as a divine energy motion of love emanating from the center in which God's spirit is the eternal fountain—and our soul dwells in such a sphere of love, relishing heavenly wisdom and knowledge. In his benevolent sphere, the Universal Master allows human intellect, empowered by the soul, to perceive particular things in a universal manner, enabling us to have a priori knowl-edge of things we never can experience on the basis of empirical knowledge. God, in fact, through the soul, channels his wisdom and knowledge to hu-mankind, drawing us toward his universality so that we may be gravitated toward his spirit, adhering to the unity in love. If Newton's law of universal gravitation vindicated that any two bodies in the universe attract each other with a force that is directly proportional to the product of their masses and inversely proportional to the square of the distance between them, then the human soul is a gravitational device secretly planted in human consciousness by God so that humankind can communicate with His spirit, even during our corporeal state of life.

IMPLICATION OF Φ

The communication with His spirit, however, can be broken if we do not obey the second principle: harmonic law with the mathematical symbol Φ named as the golden ratio or divine proportion. Later, this became known as the golden mean, developed by Aristotle to apply to human behaviors (and which will be a main discussion in later chapters in this book). In the meantime, I want to explore the mathematical significance of divine proportion—which is the preferred name over "golden ratio." The Φ is a number often encoun-tered when examining the ratios of distances in simple geometric figures such as the pentagon, pentagram, decagon, and dodecahedron. A special ratio is found when we divide a line into two parts, so that the longer part divided by the smaller part is also equal to the whole length divided by the longer part. This ratio represents universal harmony and beauty with a special number approximately equal to 1.618. To calculate the ratio, one can draw a rectangle as shown in figure 1.

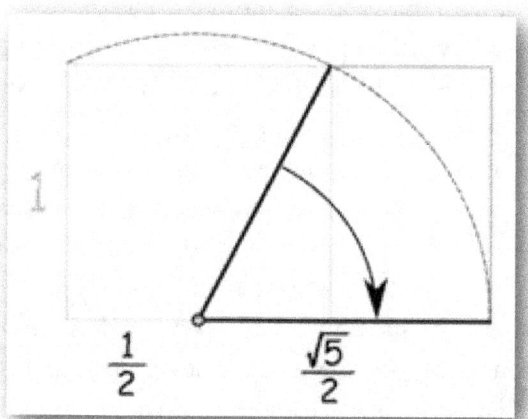

Figure 1: How to draw a rectangle for the golden ratio

Here, you draw a square (of size "1"); place a dot halfway along one side; draw a line from that point to an opposite corner (it will be √5/2 in length), and turn that line so that it runs along the square's side. Then you can extend the square to be a rectangle with the golden ratio. That rectangle above shows us a simple formula for the golden ratio. When one side is 1, the other side is

$$\varphi = \frac{1}{2} + \frac{\sqrt{5}}{2} = \frac{1 + \sqrt{5}}{2} = 1.618$$

The ancient Greeks believed that beauty consists of three components: symmetry, proportion, and harmony. They considered these properties to be natural and intrinsic to all beautiful things. Pythagoras was the first to explicitly articulate this idea. To Pythagoras, to understand beauty is to know the property of Φ.

The teachings of Pythagoras revolve around the idea that when considering the deepest level, true reality is essentially mathematical in nature. Thus,

Pythagoras believed a system of principles could be found behind numbers. One of his most basic notions revolves around the symbolism of beauty associated with the divine proportion denoted by Φ. That is, the harmony is a pleasing combination of elements that produces beauty based on the exquisite proportion prescribed by Φ. Perceptional cognition of harmony is the absence of roughness that pleases the sight, and in feeling, it evokes peaceful pleasure and happiness. The opposite of these would then be chaos, cacophony, disorder, and unhappiness.

By understanding such organizing principles, we begin to fathom divine reasoning that tries to communicate with human intellect. It appears that the cosmic principle of harmony is to be applied directly to every human behavioral rationality to maintain the same harmony as laid out for the cosmic sphere—for we are an integral part of such a large sphere. Aristotle expanded the concept of beauty of harmony into three-dimensional worlds, including human action, saying that it occurs when all parts work together in harmony so that no one part draws unjust attention to itself.

The living monument of such exquisite harmony, shining φ, is none other than the Great Pyramid of Giza, built over forty-five hundred years ago (between 2532 and 2504 BC according to radiocarbon-dating tests). To this day, it is still the largest stone monument. Among all aspects, the design of the pyramid demonstrates the geometric relationship of the celestial bodies and Earth based on the harmonic law that rules Earth in the circle of God's grace. With its original height at over 146 meters and base area of 53,065 m², the Great Pyramid of Egypt closely embodies divine proportion.

To illustrate this in more precise terms, the design of the structure consists of three-pronged geometrical principles: divine proportion (φ) and the essence of a circle in relation to its diameter, converging with the Pythagorean right triangle, which can be expressed as $a^2 = b^2 + h^2$ as shown in figure 2. It was built long before Greek civilization and still stands today as the greatest architectural achievement on Earth. Its dimensions and orientation have marveled mathematicians and astronomers for centuries, which lead us to a compelling thought: that perhaps the Great Pyramid is the ultimate symbol of the ideal world on Earth that contains the Master's thinking in terms of design. Its dimensions are based on the divine ratio (φ) as illustrated in figure 2.

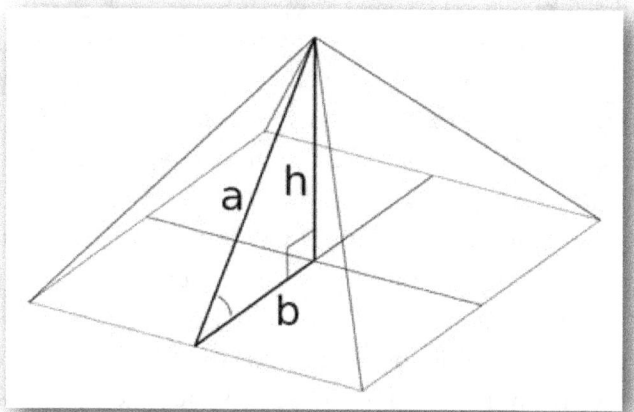

Figure 2: Mathematical configuration of a pyramid

First, let's compute hypotenuse height *a* with known height (*h* = 146.515 m) and base *b* = 115.182 m. So:

$$a\_(\text{sq.}) = 146.515 \ (\text{sq.}) + 115.182 \ (\text{sq.}) = 34{,}733$$
$$\text{and}$$
$$a = 186.369 \ m$$

Now let's prove that the Great Pyramid contains the golden ratio. Dividing slant height *a* by base gives 186.369 ÷ 15.182 = 1.61804 = φ. This proof was discovered by Kepler as shown in figure 3. Just as π is the ratio of the circumference of a circle to its diameter, φ is simply the ratio of the line segments that result when a line is divided in one very special and unique way. Even though we do not classify φ as a transcendental number like π mathematically, it cannot be written as exact fractions, as its decimal fraction expansions go on forever. (To give you an idea, the latest record is ten trillion places in computation.) Another mysterious but splendid aspect of the Great Pyramid is that it approximately squares the circle. Recall from figure 1 above that if we let each side of square be two units in length, then:

$$\text{perimeter of base} = 2 + 2 + 2 + 2 = 8 \text{ (boundary of square)}$$
$$\text{pyramid height} = \sqrt{\Phi} = 1.272 \text{ (i.e., 1.272 sq. = 1.618)}$$
$$\text{and}$$
$$\text{base} = 1+1 = 2$$

Then, for a circle with radius equal to pyramid height $\sqrt{\Phi}$:

$$\text{circumference of circle} = 2\,\pi\,\sqrt{\Phi} = 7.992$$
$$\text{(Remember the circumference being } 2\pi r.)$$

Hence, the circumference of circle results in 7.999.

The perimeter of the square and the circumference of the circle differ by less than 0.1 percent as shown in the above calculation. Thus, the Great Pyramid equals the circle. The square, with its four corners like the corners of a house represents earthly things, while the circle—perfect, endless, infinite—has often been taken to represent the divine universe. So squaring the circle symbolizes the human potential to bring terrestrial life in alignment with the divine. In more than one way, the configuration of the Great Pyramid conveys a profound message, commanding humankind to duplicate the universal kingdom on Earth: meaning a peaceful society, with harmonic law manifested in Φ.

KEPLER'S HARMONIC WORLD

A special resounding message in π is that God embraces all earthlings in His circle of grace, regardless of whether one believes in His grand spirit or not. Thus, we are not only protected by His benevolent grace with π but also encouraged to reach out for His wisdom to expand our intellect to develop a sound rationality to fulfill the purpose of harmonic law. Kepler was immensely fascinated by the Great Pyramid and, in his right triangle, recognized the implication of golden ratio converging into the Pythagoras right triangle as illustrated in figure 3.

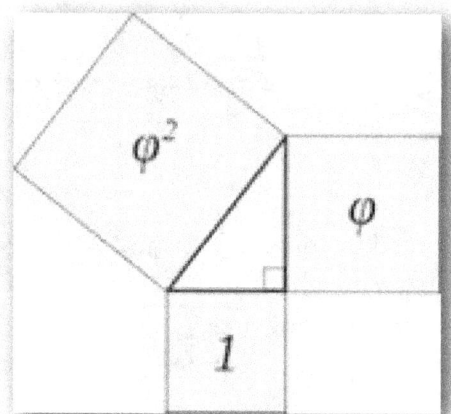

Figure3: Kepler's basic triangle

By applying the Pythagorean equation, Kepler discovered that the right triangle with sides of length *a* and *b* and hypotenuse *c* has the following relationship:

$$\varphi^2 = \varphi + 1$$

Or in the form of the Pythagorean theorem:

$$(\varphi)^2 = (\sqrt{\varphi})^2 + (1)^2.$$

Note that the circle and square have approximately the same perimeter as the Kepler triangle.

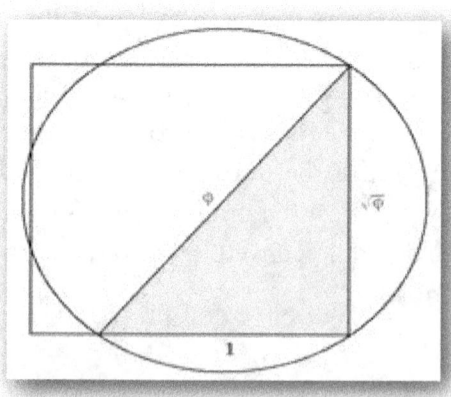

Next, let's construct a square with side length $\sqrt{\phi}$ and the circumcircle of Kepler triangle. What are the perimeters of each? Well, the square has perimeter $4\sqrt{\phi} = 5.088$ and the circumference of circumcircle has $\pi\phi = 5.083$, which is a different way of proving again the approximation of square to the circle being $\pi = 4/\sqrt{\phi}$. This is a very special mathematical equation implicating that all of humankind is necessarily embraced by God's grace (π) and that they can approximate the heavenly kingdom on Earth by obeying the harmonic law (ϕ) of heaven.

Indeed, it was Kepler who made the golden ratio and God's grace shine as jewels with the truths that Egyptians applied several thousand years before. He was exalted in discovery of universal harmony ordained by God: "It is my pleasure to taunt mortal men with the candid acknowledgment that I am stealing the golden vessels of the Egyptians to build a tabernacle to my God from them, far, far away from the boundaries of Egypt."[6] Kepler combined mathematics and the philosophy of Pythagoras in deep admiration of him. He once jokingly remarked that he might need to ask the ghost of Pythagoras for assistance with his profound work *Harmonices Mundi*, in which he draws on Euclidean geometry, Pythagorean musical, and cosmic harmony to describe the universe.

PYTHAGORAS AND COSMIC HARMONY

The discovery of the golden ratio, which appears frequently in geometry, is in fact attributed to Pythagoras, who was the first philosopher and mathematician introducing the concept of harmony. For Pythagoras, mathematics was a bridge between the visible and invisible worlds. He pursued the study of mathematics, not only as a way of understanding the nature but also as a means of turning the mind away from the physical world (which can be considered transitory and unreal) and leading it to the contemplation of eternal truth that never varies. He taught his students that by focusing on the elements of mathematics, they could calm and purify the mind and, ultimately, through disciplined effort, experience true happiness—bliss. No other messianic figure

---

6 Johannes Kepler, *Harmonices Mundi* (Harmony of the World), Book V (American Philosophical Society, 1997).

has inspired and influenced philosophers, theologians, mathematicians, and astronomers—as well as musicians, composers, poets, and architects of the Middle Ages of Europe—as Pythagoras did.

The basic tenets of Pythagoras philosophy include the following:

* the reality is mathematically describable;
* the practice of philosophy can transform the soul;
* the soul has the potential to transcend the earthly plane and unite with God; and
* the cosmos is harmonious.

Western science began with Pythagoras's belief that the universe is ultimately describable in mathematical terms, and Kepler, like other scientists of the Renaissance period, was not exempt from that belief. In his constant effort to find a precise astronomical basis for the notion of cosmic harmony, Kepler kept revisiting Pythagoras's right triangle for assistance.

It should be remembered, however, that the presence of the golden ratio goes back to early Bronze Age of human history, as seen in Egyptian, Sumerian, and Greek vases; Chinese pottery; Olmec sculptures; and Cretan and Mycenaean products. The application of such a special number in art and architecture, even before its formal discovery by Kepler, perhaps evidences that primal human cognitive instinct gravitated to this divine proportion, for it is the effusion of God's wisdom transmitted into human souls, from age to age.

It is clearly evident that both π and Φ were applied in the design of the Great Pyramid, whether the builders consciously recognized the mathematical coincidence involving π and Φ or not. We accept the historical records indicating that the first identification of Φ is attributed to Pythagoras and later to Euclid in the fifth century BC, way before Kepler rediscovered it in the sixteenth century. The name "golden ratio," however, was not coined until the eighteenth century by the German mathematician, Martin Ohm. The golden ratio (Φ) is truly a divine ratio that dictates the proportions of everything from nature's smallest building blocks, such as atoms, to the unimaginably large celestial bodies in their propagation and progression.

FIBONACCI'S GOLDEN RATIO

Contemporary mathematicians, scientists, and naturalists appreciate the aesthetic value of progression and proportion of the golden ratio developed by Leonardo Fibonacci, a brilliant mathematician of the twelfth century (1175–1250) in Italy. Each number in this sequence is simply the sum of the two preceding sums (1, 1, 2, 3, 5, 8, 13, etc.). But the sequence is not all that important; rather, it is the ratio of the adjacent sums that possesses constant proportion, roughly 1.618! So why is this number so important? Well, almost everything that has three-dimensional properties adheres to the ratio of 1.618, which has a fundamental function for the building blocks, not only of nature but also of organic bodies (including humans) to maintain the harmony. Thus, Φ, along with π, is probably the most important cosmic secret to understanding our life on Earth and the intention of the Creator—for which it was properly called the "divine proportion" by Luca Pacioli (1445–1517), a Franciscan friar. Pacioli was known mostly as a mathematician but was keenly interested in art, and he published his book, *De divina proportione (On the Divine Proportion)*, in 1509. "Divine proportion" is defined as the harmonious relation of parts to one another or to the whole, manifesting the beauty of form arising from balanced proportions. The book contains illustrations in woodcut drawings by Leonardo da Vinci.

LEONARDO DA VINCI AND VITRUVIAN MAN

Da Vinci (1452–1519) drew the illustrations of the regular five Platonic solids and other drawings that have inherent divine proportions for Pacioli's book while he lived with and took mathematics lessons from Pacioli. He called it the *sectio aurea*, which is Latin for "golden section." Da Vinci has been well known throughout the world for several centuries as one of the greatest painters of all time and perhaps the most diversely talented person who ever lived. Among all his brilliant works of art, perhaps the best illustration of divine proportion is the "Vitruvian Man." The official title of the drawing is "The proportions of the human body according to Vitruvius." The drawing depicts the correlations of the ideal human body with geometric proportions based on the treatise, *De architectura,* written by Vitruvius, a Roman architect who lived in the first century BC. Here, Vitruvius describes the human figure as being the principal source of proportion among the classical orders of architecture, thus inspiring Leonardo with a deep understanding of divine proportion. According to Vitruvius, circles and squares represented the perfect geometrical units that could be used to create ideal spaces, where the human figure is divided into the circumference of the circle in relation to π and also Φ. In his treatise, Vitruvius discusses the ideal symmetry and proportion of the human body as a symbol of a temple, since the proportions and measurements of the human body, divinely created, are perfect and correct. He therefore proposes that a properly constructed temple should reflect and relate to the parts of the human body. He notes that a human body can be symmetrically inscribed within both a circle and a square. Inspired by such an ideal description of the human body, Leonardo depicted the potential greatness of the man in his anatomical drawing, "Vitruvian Man."

The rediscovery of the geometrical proportions of the human body is considered one of the great achievements leading to European Renaissance in the fifteenth century. The "Vitruvian Man" is often used as symbol of the ideal human extended to the universe by mathematical order of intelligent design. We can see by examining the drawing that the combination of arm and leg positions actually creates two different poses: the one pose with the arms straight out with the feet together is circumscribed in the square, and the other pose with a spread-eagle posture is circumscribed in the superimposed circle. According to Pythagorean tradition, the circle represents the spiritual realm, and the square, material existence, so the human body represents the perfect combination of matter and spirit, which is reflected in the drawing. Overlapping Kepler triangle on the drawing, it epitomizes the divine proportion (Φ) by which ideal human is constructed, as shown on Figure 4.

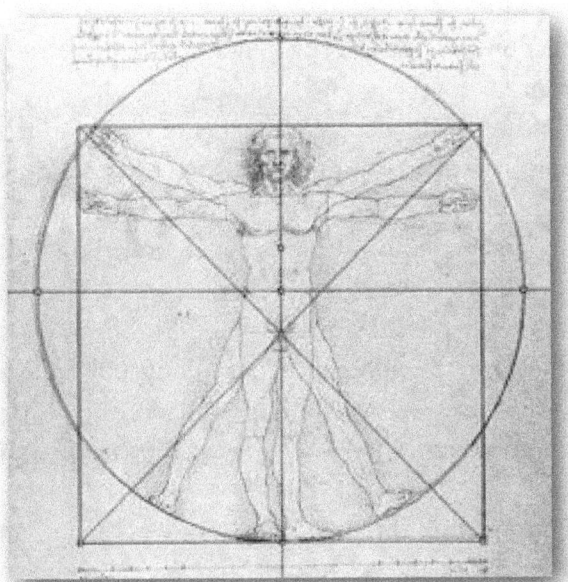

Figure 4: Kepler triangle superimposed on "Vitruvian Man"

The circle depicts the most perfect shape as the symbol for cosmic spirit, eternal and unchanging while the square is the symbol for Earth, where corporality reflects the invisible cosmic spirit. Needless to say, the proportions of the Pythagorean right triangle to the circle reflect the golden ratio and fundamental geometric patterns of the cosmic order discussed earlier with the Great Pyramid. Indeed, it is a different way of describing the Great Pyramid, by replacing an architectural structure with the human figure. Via outstretched limbs, the Vitruvian man reaches out to the celestial sphere of universe, longing for the wisdom of heaven for spiritual expansion. Differently put, he is exploring a possibility of the ideal pattern of the human world that can approximate the kingdom of heaven governed by harmonic law.

Without a doubt, the divine proportion concept has opened many doors to a deeper understanding of the beauty of human world since the Renaissance period in which Leonardo lived. The harmonic proportion and progression, the principal law of the universe, demonstrated in the Great Pyramid and rediscovered by Kepler with Pythagoras's right triangle, is abundantly displayed in the nature surrounding us. Then it is indeed a truism that everything in the universe must obey harmonic law to maintain innate proportion for equilibrium and beauty.

Mathematics, especially geometry, seems to be the most effective means of understanding and entering into the spiritual realm comprising eternal unchanging forms or ideas. In Plato's *The Republic*, Socrates said that only those well versed in geometry will be able to enter into the ideal state of mind.[7] Whether endeavoring to understand the structure of the universe or seeking the principles that underlie the organization of the cosmos as a whole, the divine proportion (φ) evokes sublime feelings in our soul as we see congruencies in nature and the universe—and the close relationship between the human intellect and the goodness of the Creator—which encourages us to strive for human potential.

The fascination with the φ is not confined just to mathematicians. Biologists, artists, musicians, architects, and myriad other researchers have pondered and contemplated the basis of its ubiquity and striking beauty. In fact, φ has inspired many thinkers of all disciplines like no other number in the history of mathematics. They have approached the same reality from different angles to search for more rounded and fuller appreciation of the universe and our place in it, for this is the cosmic law of harmony that dictates eternal equilibrium and beauty, eliciting the goodness of the human soul. Proportion's relation to beauty and goodness is stressed throughout Plato's dialogues, particularly in *The Republic* and *Philebus*,[8] citing Socrates's teaching that a man must know how to choose the midway, avoiding the extremes on either side to uphold the unity of beauty, proportion, and truth.

Aristotle, a student of Plato, eventually developed an idea of functional virtue with the purpose of human life. Aristotle reasoned that humans must have a function that sets them apart from other animals: "the function of man is to live a certain kind of life, and this activity implies a rational principle, and the function of a good man is the good and noble performance of these, and if any action is well performed it is performed in accord with the appropriate excellence: if this is the case, then happiness turns out to be an

---

7 Plato, *The Republic* Book VI, Simon & Schuster Paperback (2009)

8 Plato, *Philebus*, trans. R. Waterfield. Oxford University Press, 1998.

activity of the soul in accordance with virtue."[9] The concept was often discussed within ethical contexts to emphasize virtue. But, in truth, virtue is an attribute of beauty, as Socrates emphasized.

Beauty is an object of love and something that is to be admired and emulated. Early Greek philosophers believed that there is a close association in mathematics between beauty and truth. Thus, Greeks studied the golden ratio zealously through mathematics and philosophy. The first intellectual messianic figure in this pursuit was Pythagoras, who called himself a philosopher and lover of wisdom, believing that geometry is divine activity. He discovered harmonic law in golden ratio and, through this, introduced the concept of harmony in celestial and terrestrial spheres, even down to the action of humankind by saying, "Virtue is harmony." His influence flowed down to Socrates, Plato, and Aristotle as if the heavenly water gate had been opened, suddenly awakening the latent human intellect that can discern the beauty of harmony on Earth and in human nature per se.

Plato, as a disciple of Socrates, in his book *The Republic* highlighted Socrates's dialogue on harmony. Socrates said the goodness is in the combination of three: beauty, proportion, and truth.[10] This goodness is specifically elaborated by Aristotle for human society, with the discussion of what the virtue is and why human virtue is important by establishing the link between the concept of happiness as life's purpose and virtue as the means to achieve it. His theory of virtue is based on what we call the golden mean between the extremes, which is timeless adage in our human world.

Fortunately, we human beings are different from the rest of the mammalian family as distinguished by our reasoning power. Only humans are capable of acting according to principles and, in so doing, taking responsibility for their choices of action. That is, humans have a rational capacity to exercise to perfect the nature as human beings. For this reason, pleasure alone cannot constitute human happiness, for pleasure is what animals seek and human beings have higher capacities than animals. It is not our goal, however, to deny our physical urges or emotions but rather to channel them toward the sublime,

---

9 Aristotle, *Nicomachean Ethics*, trans. David Ross (Oxford University Press, 2009).

10 Plato, *Republic*, Book VI, trans. Benjamin Jowett, Dover Publications (2000)

expanding spiritual horizon to actualize human goodness as rational creatures. It may be said then that the proper function of humans is to live a virtuous life, and this requires rational principles in accordance with universal harmony.

INTERNAL STRUCTURE OF THE HUMAN BODY

We are created by the mega cosmic power of the universe. Once we begin to realize that we are part of the cosmic world, we begin to realize how our emotional battles on Earth are so ephemeral and meaningless, for true reality lies in the invisible world. Indeed, our corporeality on Earth none other than massive form of invisible atoms. The human body is a mass composition of atoms, with most of the mass of the body being oxygen and most of the atoms in the human body being hydrogen atoms. Hydrogen is the simplest and most abundant element in the universe. It is estimated that 90 percent of the universe is composed of hydrogen gas. Our structural body mostly is made of water, with body cells consisting of 65–90 percent water (H_2O). Water is made up of two hydrogen atoms and one oxygen atom bound by divine energy (hydrogen bonds). The structure of the electrons surrounding water is tetrahedral, strikingly resembling a construction of pyramid, assembled by the same harmonic law (Φ) witnessed in the Great Pyramid, as displayed in figure 5 below:

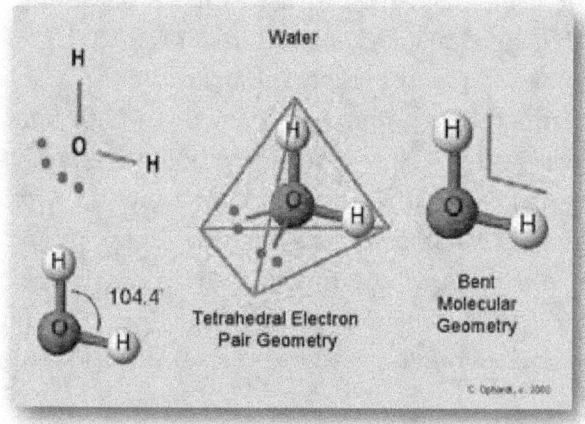

Figure 5: Geometry of water
(Source: http://www.elmhurst.edu/~chm/vchembook/206bent.html.)

In reality, the four bonds from each oxygen atom point toward the four corners of a tetrahedron centered on the oxygen atom. This basic assembly repeats itself in three dimensions to build the ice crystal. By mass, oxygen is the third most abundant element in the universe, after hydrogen and helium. All are invisible energy. This tells us that human body is created by invisible matters but held together by divine proportion (harmonic law) to become visible. As one can imagine, the harmonic law is operating within our physical body and around us, spreading the splendor of beauty in an omnipresent way.

Chapter 2

RATIONALITY
AND WISDOM

WISDOM OF THE SOUL

To me wisdom is the essential spirit of God transmitted to our soul. More specifically wisdom is spiritual nutrition transmitted to the human mind via the soul in order to develop a virtuous disposition that culminates as noble character. Wisdom awakens the comprehension of the truth, the normative perception distinguishing between the false and the true and between good and bad. It expands the capacity of the thinker to enter increasingly into the contemplation of the divine spirit, appreciating the true beauty of the universe. The wisdom helps human consciousness to harmonize more and more with the divine consciousness, as it is the spiritual product, apart from the rationality of the human mind. Thus, a virtuous mind is the manifestation of wisdom, cooperating with fellow humans in actions of compassion and humanism—what Kant calls "universal affection" and "universal respect."[11]

As one can see, our actions and deeds are the materialization of our invisible mind. In turn, our mind is shaped by character nurtured by the wisdom of the soul. Recognizing the soul as a part of the universal spirit acting as the

---

11 Immanuel Kant, *Observations on the Felling of the Beautiful and Sublime (2/217)* (Cambridge University Press, 2011).

conduit of the cosmic mind, the human mind can depend on it for betterment of judgment and reasoning. Indeed, the human soul, the chalice of wisdom, acts as a conduit of divine reason, and it is here with us in our brain to stabilize the wavering mind in a virtuous way through wisdom. It may be said that the soul is the source of the makeup of humankind, which is unique from person to person at a functional level. Nonetheless, the wisdom trickling down to each soul is universal in nature. Thus, it can ultimately unite every mind in universal consensus if all agree to rely on wisdom to solve worldly problems, purging the conflicting self-interests justified by human rationalization.

HUMAN RATIONALITY BASED ON SELF-INTEREST VERSUS WISDOM

Among all creations, so far only *Homo sapiens* have the capacity for rational thinking. In the processes of human evolution, the rational development in the brain mysteriously emerged rather than following simple physiological evolution. Practical rationality involves the individual who considers goals and, on some systematic basis, decides what is the best means or course of action to pursue in order to achieve those goals. This form of rationality can be considered pragmatic, in that it provides individuals with a way of pursuing practical ends. A rational decision, then, is one that is not just based on reason but is also optimal for achieving a goal or solving a problem. Theoretical rationality, however, begins with abstract concepts as an essential part of logical reasoning or theoretical models. These attempts try to describe, explain, or understand the world in terms of models that are constructed from observation and reasoning. These forms of rationality need not be associated with social action but are more a part of logical structures and theory. Reason and rationality are not the same: "reason" is a psychological faculty, whereas "rationality" is an optimizing strategy subsuming the reason. Having said that, the common concept of rationality exercising reason can refer to the justification of one's narrow beliefs with one's reason to believe. If one accepts that benefitting oneself is the optimal strategy, then rationality is equated with behavior that is self-interested to the point of being selfish. Generally, this type of rational thinking circles around self-interest with very marginal moral value and goodness. Reason integrates humankind's perceptions by means of forming abstractions or conceptions, thus raising human knowledge from the perceptual level (shared with animals) to the conceptual level (which humankind alone can reach). Thus we may say reason is the fountain of certain concepts and principles independent from simple perceptual level—the philosopher Immanuel Kant (1724–1804) defines it as "transcendental ideas"[12] or wisdom of God. The reason's goal is to provide unity in harmony.

This unity of reason is the wisdom of a priori, since it cannot be given through any set of experiences. As Kant states, "Pure reason, then, contains, not indeed in its speculative, but in its practical, or, more strictly, its moral use, principles of the possibility of experience, of such actions, namely, as, in accordance with ethical precepts, might be met with in the history of man."[13] It is then, in its practical but especially in its moral use, that the principles of pure reason possess objective reality that can be accepted as universal. In this case, the virtue of rationality means the recognition and acceptance of wisdom as one's only source of knowledge, one's only judge of values, and one's only guide to action.

AGE OF REASON

Many contemporary sociologists, critical theorists, and philosophers have been critiquing that human rationalization, as falsely assumed progress, has a negative and dehumanizing effect on society, moving modernity away from the central tenets of Enlightenment. As we witness individualism and a rational and scientific approach to religious, social, political, and economic issues have promoted more of secular view of the world and a general sense of progress. The proponents of the Enlightenment with supreme faith in rationality, they sought to discover and to act upon universally valid principles governing

---

12 Immanuel Kant, *Critique of Pure Reason, Part II, Transcendental Logic*, Cambridge Edition, trans. P. Guyer and Allen Wood (Cambridge University Press, 1998).
13 Ibid.

humanity, nature, and society rejecting. spiritual authority and dogmatism. Following the Age of Enlightenment, the founders of modern sociology, between the early 1800s and the early 1900s, contributed a wide range of sociological theories of great scope and ambition. They tried to produce highly systematic bodies of thought that made rational sense and that could be derived from real-world observation. Most rational choices we make, however, do not necessarily mean improvements of society in terms happiness or prosperity of all citizens.

Even on the intellectual plane that aims at a higher level of rational thinking, our intellect and ideas are often limited and ambiguous, since we cannot comprehend everything, and our judgments are not always correct because they are based on subjective reason rather than objective rationality that's universally accepted. Thus, we cannot predict the outcome of our actions with infallible certainty. We often make intellectual mistakes because human rationale is limited. This suggests that we must seek divine wisdom that is infinitely more rational than ours. Perhaps we need to understand this not merely as what one ought to do but as what ought to serve as a guide to constructing the road to wisdom that everyone should travel on and that will prevent our mind from going astray. In this way, we can regulate our conduct by temperance to self-assured imperatives, and we can postulate the transcendental reality of ourselves and free will. We must do all of this because failure to do so would be an admission that the corporeal life does not have special meaning and can even be intolerable for us quite often. Thus, Kant believed that the ultimate worth of his philosophy lay in his willingness to criticize reason in order to make room for faith. Kant's final word here offers an explanation of our persistent desire to transcend from the phenomenal realm to the noumenal. No human can seriously reconcile his or her fallible mind to a higher realm of God's spirit without humbling himself or herself to God's infinite arrangement of the cosmos. The human intellect may have the ability to organize ideas and thoughts to produce theories or create man-made laws, but it lacks enduring stability to produce the wisdom that God possesses. It is indeed sublime and awesome to watch how the Cosmic Master operates the universal energy motion with his wisdom and harmonic law, which are the natural outflow of his omniscient, omnipotent, and omnipresent nature.

As we cultivate virtuous thoughts with God's wisdom, we can increase the understanding of our mind waves, remembering Plato's adage "Know Thyself" used extensively in the dialogues of Socrates. Plato was referring to a primal wisdom of understanding how our minds operate: that is, self-awareness. Thoughts are products of our mind. If thinking is mental exercise, the thought is the mental product of our mind waves. Without wisdom, however, those mental products do not have sufficient moral value for our human society. In truth, we often do make things worse with our so-called rational thinking. In other words, the rational skill of using reason in many cases does not mean that the reason is good reason. Whereas divine rationale is the wisdom that teaches us how to solve finite problems, mirroring the grand logics of the universe that emanate the spirit of grace and compassion. We can ponder, for example, the infinite mathematical constant π that presently stands at five trillion decimal digits with no ending in sight, which compels us to think there is the eternal Master Spirit for all things modifying them in perpetual motion through many eons of evolutionary process. Indeed God's rationale belongs to the infinite universe. It is mathematically proven that we cannot square the circle due to the fact that π is an infinite number. Therefore, it was determined that π is a transcendental number. As you can guess, the circles we freely draw are never perfect because of the divine nature of π. It is thus not surprising when Georg Cantor (1845–1918), German mathematician of the nineteenth century, equated the absolute infinity with God.[14] Cantor believed that Absolute Infinity exists only in the mind of God. But he argued that God instilled the concept of numbers, both finite and transfinite, into the mind of man. Cantor frequently appealed to their existence as eternal ideas in the mind of God as the basis for the existence of the transfinite in the mind of man. With Cantor's postulation I can assume God made it plain by placing within our brain structure the soul that allows us to communicate with divine consciousness and serves as the faculty for self-examination.

---

14 Joseph Dauben, *Georg Cantor: His Mathematics and Philosophy of the Infinite* (Harvard University Press, 1979).

HUMAN CONSCIOUSNESS

Consciousness, according to Western science, has its roots in the brain, which in turn is seated in the forebrain—the highly developed frontal lobe. The frontal lobe is associated with higher-level functions such as self-control, planning, logic, and abstract thought, essentially making up the uniqueness of the human mind as distinguished from other mammals. This frontal brain is the hub of the reasoning capacity of the human mind. Thus, one can surmise that consciousness is a broad spectrum of various manifestations of mind waves operated by the large number of neurons in the frontal brain. The number of ways information is conveyed by neurons in the brain is vast. We label these "thoughts."

DIVINITY IN HUMAN CONSCIOUSNESS

The first philosopher to discuss this consciousness was René Descartes (1596–1650), who laid the foundation for seventeenth-century rationalism. Descartes proposed that consciousness resides within an immaterial domain he called *res cogitans* (the realm of thought),[15] in contrast to the domain of material things, which he called *res extensa* (the realm of extension). Descartes's *cogitans* refers to the "thinking and thoughts" that are part of our intellect—our capacity for rational thought. He is best known for the philosophical statement: *"Cogito ergo sum"* ("I think; therefore I am"). Descartes shifted the focus in philosophy from God to the subject, hinting that the starting point for knowledge lies in the human thinker and human reasoning. But he confessed how fallible the human mind is: "I am indeed amazed when I consider how weak my mind is and how prone to error."[16]

Human consciousness is inescapably finite, gravitated toward earthly life. It receives its enjoyments in the corporeal world. The human consciousness inveterately insists there is nothing more important than earthly joy. Human consciousness tries to convince a man or woman that God is somewhere else,

---

15 Rene Descartes, *Meditations on First Philosophy,* trans. J Cottingham (Cambridge University Press, 1986).

16 Ibid.

having nothing to do with his or her daily life affairs. A man (or woman) may say he (or she) does not lose anything by not believing in God. Atheists do not care for the divine reality, the existence of God either in heaven or in their day-to-day earthly lives. But when we aspire to divine wisdom, God is inspiring us to cherish divine thoughts transpired to our soul. His divine ideas compel us to think that there is a divine purpose and divine ideal beyond corporeality. In human consciousness, there is no purpose beyond mortal life, no sublime goal. In divine consciousness, there is always a goal, and this goal is always transcending itself. This happens because divine consciousness is constantly transcending and expanding.

The divine consciousness is limitless and infinite, but even in this infinity, God is not static essence, being always in progression. In the divine consciousness, everything is constantly expanding and growing into higher and more fulfilling enlightenment. When projecting one's consciousness into the realms of divine consciousness, one is defying Earth's gravity, reaching out for grand and noble ideas. The wisdom, which is the source of human virtues, most importantly inspires us to draw closer to the invisible world, strengthening our affinity with divine consciousness. In the beginning, the thoughts of God may be mere concept, but over the course of time, humankind can cognitively acknowledge a dynamic presence of His grace and compassion in human consciousness.

When we sense God, the things physically revealed are all of a sudden so beautiful, consistent with invisible reality. They also look very reasonable in a sublime way, while human rationality alone without faith could never see them that way. Faith acts as an umbilical cord that brings spiritual sustenance to our soul quenching its deep longings, and it affirms the basic purpose and meaning of our being here on Earth. Faith does not contradict human intellect or reasoning ability but complements them. The faith in the invisible reality is a fundamental quality required by any human in his or her pursuit of divine ideas. A ceaseless quest for divine ideas with faith would be able to touch a splendor of heavenly knowledge—we may call it scientific knowledge. The modern science could not have yielded its bounty of fruits without this profound faith in the invisible world.

FAITH AND SCIENCE

As Kant describes, "Science presupposes the goal of discovering the greatest possible completeness and systematics subsuming objects and events under the most all-encompassing laws.[17] Take electrons, for example—forever invisible, but they are the fundamental units of the visible world. In the microcosmic spaces surrounding and separating these subatomic particles, invisible forces determine solidity and fluidity, which generate the marvels of light and heat, and constitute the secrets of electricity. No one doubts that the modern marvels of science come from this invisible world. The close association between matter and energy suggests that the laws of the invisible world are repeated identically in the laws of the visible world.

To illustrate the point, in the study of physics (the branch of science that studies matter and its motion through space and time), scientists focus on concepts such as energy and force. Physics is one of the fundamental sciences, because the study influences other natural sciences (like biology, geology, etc.) in obeying the laws of physics. According to physics, energy and the fundamental forces of nature govern the interactions between particles and physical existence of mass. While astronomy studies celestial bodies and their interactions in space (such as the life and characteristics of stars and galaxies), chemistry studies the composition, structure, and properties of matter, with its chief focus on atoms and molecules, and their interactions and transformations. For example, the properties of the chemical bonds formed between atoms create chemical compounds. As studies progress, modern chemistry delves into the involvement of electrons and various forms of energy in photochemical reactions, oxidation-reduction reactions, and changes in phases of matter. Thus, it is obvious that physical science is the search for invisible reality. In this invisible region, we need an eye for the unseen and faith in truth, which goes hand in hand with reason. The word "faith" does not have a tangible property, except for a conviction of the holder in spiritual maturity. The unshakable faith without abandonment of human rationality receives divine rationality through the wisdom of God. This type of rationality can be called a priori knowledge, or intuition. Numerous scientific geniuses with unyielding faith eventually brought heavenly knowledge

---

17 Kant, *Critique of Pure Reason, Part II*, Chapter 1.

to Earth, helping to expand humankind's understanding of the universe. For example, Giordano Bruno (1548–1600), who is portrayed as a hero and martyr of modern science, proclaimed that God "is the inner principle of all movement, the one Identity which fills the all and enlightens the universe." He expressed his conviction that everything is contained in this principle. Where, then, should we look for God?, Bruno answered: "In the unchangeable laws of nature, in the light of the sun, in the beauty of all that springs from the bosom of Mother Earth, in the sight of unnumbered stars which shine in the skirts of space, and which live and feel and think and magnify the powers of this Universal Principle." He then proceeded to explain how this knowledge could be acquired. "Within every man," he said, "there is a soul-flame, kindled at the sun of thought, which lends us wings whereby we may approach the sun of knowledge." The soul of man, he affirmed, is the only God there is because "This principle in man moves and governs the body, is superior to the body, and cannot be constrained by it."[18]

Indeed, the real "self" of humankind is the soul. Bruno's profound faith led him to the startling discovery that stars are other suns with their own planets and our Earth planet moves around the sun and receives light and heat from it. He claimed that space is filled with an infinite number of solar systems and that each has a central sun, around which planets revolve. In fact, in Bruno's philosophy, nothing stands still—that is, everything is in motion, from the smallest atom to the largest star system. Bruno was not a mathematician, and he was not an astronomer. He was a member of the Dominican clergy, and he experienced the divine revelation that infused cosmological theories into his thoughts. Bruno's divine intuition of the infinite universe picked up where Copernicus left off, and his unitary concept of nature found admiration by very important philosophers/scholars, such as Spinoza, Jacobi, and Hegel. While his overall contribution to the birth of modern science is still unfolding, Bruno's concept of multiple universes is viewed by some scientists as a forerunner of quantum mechanics. Some believe Bruno was

---

18 Giordano Bruno, *On the Infinite, Universe, and Worlds (De l'Infinito, Universo, e Mondi),* trans. Scott Gosnell (CreateSpace Independent Publishing Platform, 2014)

one of the precursors to Sir Isaac Newton's (1643–1727) theory of place and absolute space.

Newton's conception of the physical world provided a stable model of the natural world that would reinforce stability and harmony in the universe, while Bruno believed that the universe is homogenous. In Bruno's cosmology, space and time are infinite, and the universe has planetary systems evenly distributed throughout. Furthermore, he believed that matter is intelligent and made up of discrete atoms. He felt that every part of the universe—mineral, plant, and animal—has a soul, and that all souls are akin. Needless to say, Bruno's faith in God and the universe led him to expand his horizon of thoughts far beyond the traditional idea of God maintained by religionists, and we witnessed more discoveries by Newton, Faraday, and Einstein in later periods with the same strength of faith. Indeed, these faithful souls became the fertile grounds for divine ideas, furthering human civilization with scientific developments and technological advances that we now enjoy in the modern world.

The whole scheme of the invisible and visible worlds is that they are two provinces of one kingdom. God is eternally invisible to human eyes, but human intellect can infer God's existence by contemplating the geometric law of the circle. In other words, our intellect can acknowledge that infinite π is God's eternal compassion, which encircles us, albeit invisible. In this case, only faith can lead the soul to see the invisible. There are things we see with our eyes for mainly physiological survival, but there is a spiritual eye that can capture rich views of the invisible world. These pictures are much more beauteous than anything we can see in corporeality. The things that are visible to us are only temporal in nature, whereas those things invisible are eternal truths that make up the true reality of the universe. Without faith, we are lost in the dark; however, with faith, we participate in the divine world manifested by the beauty of harmony.

Within the divine universe, grace is an expression of God's compassion toward humankind. Grace is the unconstrained expression of love and kindness. While grace itself has the power to strengthen our soul, it cannot stay active in our soul unless we seek God's wisdom to be able to discern what is truly good and evil. And of course, the more we enter into deep and frequent contemplation of the divine essence, the more mature the soul becomes and the nobler we become as our spirit matures. Undoubtedly, God's grace empowers the human soul to develop virtuous character with his compassion, the widest ocean in which grace flows. The cosmic law of harmony commands humankind to remain in divine grace in his circular universe of love (π) by expanding human goodness. The more we expand the goodness in human interactions, the more we will be secured in his infinite universe of grace. The heavenly rewards are abundant when goodness flows in harmony among humanity.

For instance, a peaceful welfare state, where wealth is equitably distributed for everyone's comfort and happiness, would flourish and prosper in timeless beauty, as it demonstrates well-balanced harmony. On the opposite side of this scenario, in a capitalistic society with excess materialistic greed devoid of humanism and compassion, an inevitable doom would befall it for rupturing the universal harmony established by divine will. We therefore can postulate that there is an omniscient, omnipotent God who ordained the human world, as well as nature, with harmonic law and rewards us for our virtue. We should be reminded that virtue is a necessary human quality for happiness. This virtue equally applies to all levels of human interactions, individuals, groups of a society, nations, and the entire planet Earth.

In conclusion, I argue that the human rationality that dehumanizes and mechanizes societies, taking advantage of technological advancements without paying vigilance to the principles of human virtue, will not be able to hold modern comfort brought about by scientific knowledge.

Chapter 3

HUMAN VIRTUE AND
WORLD RELIGIONS

ARISTOTLE'S INTELLECTUAL VIRTUE

A virtue is a quality deemed to be the highest moral quality and thus is valued as a foundation of good moral being. To put it differently, virtue is a pattern of thought and behavior based on high moral standards. In Aristotle's sense, virtue is excellence at being human, a skill that helps a person survive, thrive, form meaningful relationships, and find happiness. Learning virtue is usually difficult at first but becomes easier with practice over time until it becomes a habit.

For Aristotle, all ethics are aimed at happiness, and true happiness occurs when one acts in accord with virtue. In fact, he says that happiness is the very end of human nature.[19] To account for this, Aristotle divides the ethical life into two parts: intellectual virtue and moral virtue. Intellectual virtue is most closely associated with humans' rational nature. For Aristotle, the highest being of such intellectual virtue is the Prime Mover (God), for it is purely spiritual and intellectual. The activity of God is thought: "thought-thinking-thought."[20]

---

19 Aristotle, *Nicomachean Ethics,* trans. Robert C. Bartlett and Susan D. Collins (Chicago:University of Chicago Press 2011)
20 Aristotle, *Metaphysics,* trans. Hugh Larson (London: Penquin Books, 2004)

Aristotle believed that the Prime Mover exists necessarily, and it does not depend on anything else for existence. Humankind, as an image of this divine being, is called to ponder its (God's) nature and aspire to imitate the purity of its (God's) thought. Thus, intellectual virtue is activity aimed at contemplating the divine, and in that, it achieves happiness.

MORAL VIRTUE BY ARISTOTLE

Moral virtue, on the other hand, is something entirely human. It does not take for its object in the divine Prime Mover but functions in the corporeal world. Moral virtue is constituted by activities belonging to our composite nature. For instance, the civic virtue of political community belongs to this category. Aristotle says that whereas virtue of thinking needs teaching, experience, and time, virtue of character (moral virtue) comes about as a consequence of following the right habits. According to Aristotle, the potential for this virtue is by nature in humans, but whether virtues come to be present or not is not determined by human nature but practice.[21] It is obvious that the happiness afforded by morally virtuous action is altogether different than the happiness of intellectual contemplation. While contemplation seeks a divinely bestowed happiness, moral virtue results in human flourishing, or *Eudaimonia* (happiness). It is notable in Aristotle's teaching a strong echo of God that reverberates throughout his notion of what it means for humans to act in accordance with their composite nature. In other words, to understand what Aristotle intended by the moral life requires one to take into consideration his idea of God. His concept of virtue and morality is rich with appreciation of God (divine Spirit) as the cause of all.

Aristotle had a profound influence on philosophical and theological thinking in the Islamic and Jewish traditions as well in the Middle Ages, and his philosophy continues to influence Christian theology, especially the scholastic tradition of the Catholic Church. Saint Thomas Aquinas described him as the Christian Aristotle and the prince of theologians. Since humankind is primarily a rational animal—that is, reasonable and capable of thinking and pondering—Aristotle's idea of moral virtue must certainly take this into account. If living in harmony

---

21 Aristotle, *Nicomachean Ethics*.

with other human beings requires one to know what it means to be a human being, understanding the model of rationality per se is an important thing.

CHRISTIAN PRINCIPLES BY THOMAS AQUINAS

Saint Thomas Aquinas (1225–74) was an Italian Catholic philosopher and theologian in the scholastic tradition, known as "Doctor Angelicus" and "Doctor Universalis." His theology was profoundly influenced by Aristotle's ideas on human virtue and rational thinking, and he became the most famous proponent of "natural theology"—theology based on reason and ordinary experience. (Natural theology is distinguished from "revealed theology," which is based on scripture and spiritual experiences of various kinds.)

The Roman Catholic Church still holds the view of natural law set forth by Aquinas. The natural law refers to the use of reason to analyze human nature (both social and personal) and deduce binding rules of moral behavior. This view is also shared by some Protestant churches. Humans are capable of discerning the difference between good and evil because they have a conscience—judgment of the intellect that distinguishes right from wrong. Conscience usually is linked to a morality inherent in all humans. Similarly according to Hindu philosophy, conscience is the label given to attributes that generate knowledge about virtues and vices, which a soul acquires from the completion of acts and consequent accretion of karma over many lifetimes.

In Aquinas's theology, much of the structure of Aristotle and a great deal of his own insight are combined. Aristotle and Aquinas have many similar thoughts on the way the human person should live. Both of them believe that humans are rational beings. They also believe that because humans are rational, they can follow their instincts and live a life of moral goodness. Aquinas, however, believed that God is the core spirit leading human beings to a rational, moral life, whereas Aristotle believed that being moral is naturally inherent in human beings. Although they had different views as to why human beings should want to live a good life, they both agreed that the one thing humans *should* strive for is happiness (*Eudaimonia*).

In Aquinas's view, happiness may be considered in two ways. One is commensurate with our human nature and therefore a happiness obtainable by the use of our native powers of mind and will. But this worldly happiness is rather enjoyment in satisfying worldly desire. The other is immeasurably higher, surpassing nature and secured only from God by the merciful communication of His own divinity. To make it possible to attain this higher destiny in the beatific vision, we must have new principles of activity, which are called "theological virtues," because their objective is God and not, as in moral virtues, merely things that lead to God—because they are infused in the mind and will by God alone, as opposed to the habits acquired by personal exercise, and because they would never be known to us except through divine revelation. Aquinas, being an Aristotelian, agreed with many of the ways in which Aristotle viewed the human person. However, where he diverged was his belief in God. He took the teachings of Aristotle and added God to them so that there would be more acceptance of them within Christian society.

In Aquinas's theology, the soul is the substantial form of the body, which gives humankind all that is properly human and places him or her essentially into the natural order—and which gives the same man or woman all that is properly divine and puts him or her habitually into the family of God. Thus, according to Aquinas, the soul is the foundation of natural existence. St. Thomas Aquinas defines virtue as a good habit bearing on activity which stands in a special relation to the soul, whether in the natural order or elevated to the divine life by grace.

The soul is the source of all our activities. Faculties (i.e., three-fold division of the vegetative, the sensitive, and the intellectual/Rational faculties) are the proximate sources built into the soul by nature; habits are still more immediate principles added to the faculties, either by personal endeavor or by supernatural insemination from God. Consequently, the soul helps the man or woman; faculties support the soul, and habits help the faculties. Not every habit is a virtue, but only one that so improves and perfects a rational faculty as to incline it toward good—good for the faculty, for the will, and for the whole man or woman in terms of his or her ultimate destiny. On the one hand, the "instilled virtues" are independent of the process. They are directly obtained from God in the operative faculties of a human and differ mainly from the acquired because they do not imply the human effort that determines the faculty to a particular kind of activity—namely, facility induced by repetition. God himself pours in the "infused virtues," not by compulsion or overriding the free will of man, but without dependence on us, which Saint Augustine of Hippo (354–430 AD) says, "are produced in us by God without our assistance." Infused virtues are supernatural gifts, freely conferred through the merits of Christ, and they raise the activity of those who possess them to the divine level, to a share in the life of God. They represent supernatural wisdom precisely because they transcend the natural capacities of the human mind and will. The wisdom nurtures the human mind to expand consciousness so that it can perceive the fact that human intellect alone cannot reach perfection. In turn, virtue is the sublime application of knowledge and wisdom to the worldly affairs of humankind.

On the other hand, a moral virtue, by definition, avoids extremes. A well-known feature of Aristotle's ethics, which deeply influenced Aquinas, is the theory that each of the moral virtues is a mean between excess and defect. But when the faith is absent, there is no question of limiting the practice of moral virtue by reason alone. First, we must have light for the mind, both of principles and practical knowledge, and then rectitude for the will to have it tend naturally to the good as defined for us by reason. Faith sublimates reason as the standard of moderation, and just as prior to faith there are acquired virtues commensurate with reason to assist the natural mind and will in the performance of morally good acts, so with the advent of faith there should be corresponding supernatural virtues commensurate to the light of faith to assist the elevated human faculties in the performance of supernaturally good actions in the moral order.

Here, if anywhere, the familiar dictum that "grace does not destroy but builds upon nature" is eminently true. With reason enlightened by faith, the scope of virtuous operation is extended to immeasurably wider horizons. By the same token, faith furnishes motives of which reason would never conceive, and theological compassion offers inspiration that surpasses anything found in nature. The primary object of compassion is love of God. Love of God is not authentic unless we love others. Love is the new commandment of Christ as the greatest of all virtues. Aquinas and Aristotle both recognize that virtue is not its own reward and has little meaning apart from an ultimate goal. The ultimate goal is happiness. Virtue alone brings continuous and complete happiness, because it is the activity of the highest part of humankind's complete nature and of that part that is least dependent on externals. A man or woman is virtuous because his or her actions correspond to an objective norm, which for Aristotle was knowable by reason and for Aquinas by reason and faith in God.

Aristotle almost identified morally good conduct with an aesthetic mean between opposite extremes. For Aristotle, a human was basically virtuous because he or she displayed a beautiful balance in his or her moral actions, like the harmony displayed in a work of art. Aquinas saw the good man with a vision that Aristotle didn't quite extend. What was missing in Aristotle were two dimensions of morality that the Christian religion brought into full light: that internal dispositions and their consequent actions are virtuous (not mainly because of an aesthetic harmony of agent, conduct, and environment, but because they advance their possessor in the direction of his or her final destiny to eternal life after death) and that virtue is more than a reasonable balance between behavioristic extremes since it postulates a primal obligation to divine God, whose will is manifest in conscience and faith, and to whom obedience is due as humankind's Creator.

ISLAMIC PRINCIPLE OF WISDOM

Al-Ghazali (1058–1111) has been referred to by historians as the single most influential Muslim after the Islamic prophet Muhammad. Al-Ghazali bitterly denounced Aristotle, Socrates, and other Greek writers as nonbelievers, and labeled those who employed their methods and ideas as corrupters of the Islamic faith. However, Al-Ghazali had an important influence on both Muslim philosophers and Christian medieval philosophers. Margaret Smith writes in her 1944 book, *Al-Ghazali: The Mystic*: "There can be no doubt that Ghazali's works would be among the first to attract the attention of these

European scholars." Then she emphasizes: "The greatest of these Christian writers who was influenced by Ghazali was St. Thomas Aquinas," who made a study of the Arabic writers and admitted his indebtedness to them. Aquinas studied at the University of Naples where the influence of Arab literature and culture was predominant at the time.

Al-Ghazali's influence on Islam has been compared to the works of Aquinas on Christian theology, but the two differed greatly in methods and beliefs. Whereas Al-Ghazali rejected non-Islamic philosophers such as Aristotle and saw it fit to discard their teachings on the basis of their "unbelief," Aquinas embraced them and incorporated ancient Greek and Latin thoughts into his own philosophical writings. Al-Ghazali began his discussion of virtues with wisdom, while Aristotle began with rational thinking rather than wisdom.

To Al-Ghazali, wisdom is the virtue of the human soul. Since the human soul has two faculties, theoretical and practical, there are two types of wisdom corresponding to them: namely, theoretical wisdom and practical wisdom. Theoretical wisdom is concerned with the knowledge of God and His attributes. This knowledge is true wisdom because the specific aim of theoretical wisdom is the knowledge of God and not simply knowledge per se. Al-Ghazali defines wisdom in his book *The Supreme Purpose* as the most excellent thing through the best of science. But, he adds, the best knowledge is knowledge of God, for the most excellent thing is God. Whoever knows all things but does not know God does not deserve to be called wise, whereas he who knows God is wise even if his knowledge of the rest of the formal science is lacking.

According to Al-Ghazali, true wisdom is knowledge of God. But it is not the highest virtue. Unlike Aristotle, who considered the highest virtue as a form of the most perfect knowledge, Al-Ghazali regards wisdom, in his view, the most perfect knowledge, as important only insofar as it leads to the love of God. The love of God is higher than mere knowledge of him, although it comes as a result of such knowledge. In the end, Al-Ghazali and Aristotle agree that the virtue of moral wisdom is independent of theoretical wisdom but rational in that it engages in deliberation.

BUDDHISM AND COMPASSION

Buddhism deals with the human mind. Every action we perform leaves an imprint, or potential, on our very subtle mind, and each karmic potential eventually gives rise to its own effect. Our mind is like a field, and performing actions is like sowing seeds in that field. Positive or virtuous actions sow the seeds of future happiness, and negative or nonvirtuous actions sow the seeds of future suffering. This definite relationship between actions and their effects—virtue causing happiness and nonvirtue causing suffering—is known as the law of karma. An understanding of the law of karma is the basis of Buddhist morality. The goals of humankind are to cultivate both wisdom and compassion; then these qualities together will enable one ultimately to attain enlightenment, which is synonymous with spiritual union with God.

There are three trainings or practices that all Buddhists abide by: virtue, good conduct, and morality. This is based on two fundamental principles: the principle of equality and the principle of reciprocity, which is the golden rule in Christianity: to do onto others as you would wish them to do unto you. In fact, this golden rule is found in all major religions. Buddhism emphasizes the practice of virtue (a practice of nonextremism), a path of moderation away from the extremes of self-indulgence and self-mortification. This description of virtue is remarkably similar to the ideas of Aristotle and Aquinas, who emphasize habit in a mean between excess and defect. Developing virtue is the path to wisdom, which in turn leads to personal freedom. Mental development also strengthens and controls our mind; this helps us maintain good conduct. Discernment, insight, wisdom, and enlightenment are the real heart of Buddhism, called *prajna*. Wisdom will emerge if your mind is pure and calm.

Therefore, Buddhism emphasizes meditation to achieve a higher state of consciousness, which promotes good thoughts and conquers evil thoughts. Meditation is fundamentally concerned with two themes: transforming the mind and using it to explore itself and other universal phenomena. The mind is neither physical nor a byproduct of purely physical processes but a formless continuum that is a separate entity from the body. When the body disintegrates at death, the mind does not cease. Although our superficial conscious mind ceases, it does so by dissolving into a deeper level of consciousness, called "the very subtle mind," or "universal mind." In broad terms, the universal mind is equivalent to God's mind, although Buddhism does not identify it so.

MIDDLE PATH AND HUMAN VIRTUE

In the East, Buddha (sixth century BC) also taught the equivalence to golden mean as guidance to ideal human actions: "There is addiction to indulgence of sense-pleasures, which is low, coarse, the way of ordinary people, unworthy, and unprofitable; and there is addiction to self-mortification, which is painful, unworthy, and unprofitable. Avoiding both these extremes, the Tathagata (the Perfect One) has realized the Middle Path; it gives vision, gives knowledge, and leads to calm, to insight, to enlightenment and to Nirvana. And what is that Middle Path realized by the Tathagata...? It is the Noble Eightfold path, and nothing else, namely: right understanding, right thought, right speech, right action, right livelihood, right effort, right mindfulness and right concentration."[22]

Certainly, Aristotle's golden mean and Buddha's middle way are the keys to human happiness and maintaining harmony in societies. Aristotle's idea of virtue is centered around a person's character. But improving it on an individual level also improves society by and large.

In a nutshell, human virtue is the fulfillment of heavenly wisdom flowing from the divine mind and defined as goodness—for goodness is the ultimate bedrock of virtue. If we subtract goodness from human nature, the rest adds

---

22 Buddha, *Dhammacakkappavattana Sutta: Setting in Motion the Wheel of Truth*, trans. Piyadassi Thera. The Setting in Motion of the Wheel of the Dharma Sutra (or Promulgation of the Law Sutra) is a Buddhist text that is considered to be a record of the first teaching given by Gautama Buddha after he attained enlightenment. According to tradition, the Buddha gave this teaching in Sarnath, India, to the "five ascetics," his former companions with whom he had spent six years practicing austerities. The main topic of this sutra is the Four Noble Truths, which are the central teachings of Buddhism that provide a unifying theme, or conceptual framework, for all of Buddhist thought. This sutra also introduces the Buddhist concepts of the Middle Way, impermanence, and dependent origination. (PediaPress-Wikipedia Book, 1999)

little value to distinguish humans from other mammals. To put it differently, the implication of "God's image" in humans is nothing other than the goodness that should be practiced through virtuous actions if harmony and happiness are desired in the corporeal world. Aristotle thought that all human beings wanted happiness (Eudaimonia) more than anything else. Then he emphasized virtue, a product of wisdom, as a necessary requisite for the ultimate goal of human life—happiness. For Aristotle, Eudaimonia involves activity, exhibiting virtue in accordance with reason, viewing that reason is unique to human beings, and that the ideal function of a human being is the fullest exercise of reason. Then he quickly adds that the pursuit of happiness is an activity of the soul in accordance with perfect virtue that can be exercised by human rationality.

The question Aristotle seeks to answer in his lectures in *Nicomachean Ethics* is "What is the ultimate purpose of human existence and [the] goal for which he should direct all activities?" He is saying that an ultimate end must be self-sufficient and final: "that which is always desirable in itself and never for the sake of something else."[23] Further, it must be attainable by man. Saint Thomas Aquinas (1224–74), on the other hand, says that perfect happiness is not possible in this lifetime, but he goes on to say that that we can achieve a kind of "imperfect happiness"[24] here on Earth depending on the actualization of one's natural faculties. The highest faculty the human being possesses is reason. Thus, we can achieve happiness in this life in proportion to the level of truth accessible to reason through which the best human functionality can be carried out. Aquinas identified the goal of human existence as union and eternal fellowship with God, which implies the spiritual awareness of divine grace and harmonic law (π and Φ).

It is easy for our minds, without spiritual harness, to be tempted by a desire for possessions, pleasure, or fame, believing that these will lead to happiness. Contemplating the golden mean and necessary human virtue, it is not hard for us to perceive that the excess desire of wealth accumulation,

---

23 Aristotle, *Nicomachean Ethics*, Book I, trans. Robert C. Bartlett and Susan D. Collins (University of Chicago Press 2011)

24 Aqainas, *Summa contra Gentiles*, Book 3, trans. Vernon J. Bourke (University of Notre Dame Press, 1975).

hedonism, or self-centeredness is not aligned with the human faculty of reason. In this light, an extreme capitalism that creates economic inequality today is deemed a serious default void of human virtue, leaving the world far from happiness. We are facing today alarming statistics of wealth inequality in many nations, and the gap between the rich and poor continues to grow, while the growth of the world population is only creating more poor. (See chapter 10 in this book.) An excess wealth accumulation by a small number of the population without equitable redistribution measure can create chaos, opposing the force of harmony—just as Aristotle pointed out that dispro-portionate elements constitute disharmony in society. It is clear that when the divine proportion (Φ) is violated by human volition, we end up forfeiting the privilege of universal happiness and peace granted to humankind by the grace of God.

The purpose of the divine laws of π and Φ is clearly to maintain the sublime beauty and harmony of the universe, thus applying to human inter-actions equally. That is, by observing the golden mean and exercising virtue, the spirit of humankind can conjoin with the divine Spirit. The circle, being the most fundamental truth of the universe—with no definable beginning or ending, and every part of the circumference equidistant from the center—is parallel to the equitable society intended by God. No other geometric figure has all its points equidistant from its center as the circle. Pi is defined as the ratio of a circle's circumference to its diameter, or equivalently as the ratio of the circumference to twice the radius. Radii, then, are the arms of God widely open in celestial and terrestrial spheres, one arm leading human intellect to rationality and the other arm embracing everything and everyone with equal compassion and love.

The infinity of the kingdom of God and his equal compassion for all are expressed in the geometrical circle through π. Perhaps a perfect circle may not be possible with human intellect as it is; nonetheless, we have mathematical hints that say the human intellect can conceive the wisdom of God to build a civilized world where all of us are equally happy by exercising virtue together as one unit of the "image of God."

HINDUISM

The practices and goals of Buddhism and Hinduism have more similarities than differences. Hinduism conceives of the whole world as a single family that deifies the one truth, the one God. Therefore, it accepts all forms of beliefs and dismisses labels of distinct religions that would imply a division of identity. Hence, Hinduism is devoid of the concepts of apostasy, heresy, and blasphemy. Hinduism is not a homogeneous, organized system. Many Hindus are devoted followers of Shiva or Vishnu, whom they regard as the only true God, while others look inward to the divine self (atman). But most recognize the existence of Brahman, the unifying principle and Supreme Reality behind all that is. Hinduism has no founder or date of origin. The authors and dates of most Hindu sacred texts are unknown. Scholars describe modern Hinduism as the product of religious development in India that spans nearly four thousand years, making it the oldest-surviving world religion. Indeed, as seen above, Hindus regard their religion as eternal (sanatama). About 80 percent of India's population regard themselves as Hindus, and 30 million more Hindus live outside of India. There are a total of 900 million Hindus worldwide, making Hinduism the third-largest religion (after Christianity and Islam). Most Hindus believe that the spirit or soul—the true self of every person, called the ātman—is eternal.

There was an important contribution made by the Nyāya school of logic in its methodology to prove the existence of God, making the logical inference that the universe is an effect, and it ought to have a Creator. The initial exponent of the Nyāya philosophy was Mahārṣi Akṣapāda Gautama, who had first propounded the philosophy by authoring the Nyāya sutras. The Nyāya sutra was compiled around 550 BC. This methodology is based on a system of logic that subsequently has been adopted by the majority of the other Indian schools, orthodox or not. It's comparable to how Western science and philosophy can be said to be largely based on Aristotelian logic. However, Nyāya differs from Aristotelian logic in that it is more than logic in its own right. Its followers believed that obtaining valid knowledge was the only way to obtain release from suffering. Thus Nyaya is both philosophical and religious in addition to logic.

HUMAN SOUL AS THE SOURCE OF RELIGIOUS BELIEF

I've illustrated briefly the differences among major religions adopted by a large number of believers in today's world. The comparison reveals that the major thrust in their dogmatic arguments are very minor in contrast to the striking similarity in the bigger concerns about human happiness. All of them are aimed at human virtue that produces happiness. They all agree upon the function of human virtue and its relationship to the higher reality of God's wisdom. Thus, religions are good instruments that help believers to refine their soul to practice human virtues.

Religious beliefs are deep rooted in the human soul and will remain a major part of human society as long as people seek something bigger than themselves for spiritual comfort and happiness, and as long as it makes a difference in people's lives—to help change behavior and attitudes from bad to good and from good to better. When a large population is in agreement, a religion tends to represent a collective cultural system, which in turn establishes a specific dogma relating humanity to spirituality and, to a large degree, to moral values. Religious beliefs tend to derive morality, ethics, religious laws, and/or a preferred lifestyle from ideas about the universe and human nature mirroring the religion. Often, unfortunately, such beliefs are so confined in their own unique dogma and zealotry that an analogy of blind men describing an elephant seems quite appropriate. In essence, every religionist worships and yearns for the same divinity (whom we may call God): omniscience, omnipotence, and omnipresence.

Thus, our views on various religions should be more tolerant and accepting than rejecting or condemning. Everyone has the right to protect one's faith and must respect one another's religion, as long as no one tries to argue about another's belief. Unfortunately, throughout human history religious war has been the most brutal and abhorrent type of war—caused by, or justified by, religious differences. In the modern world, it can involve one state of established religion against another state of a different religion, or a different sect within the same religion. It can involve a religiously motivated group attempting to spread its faith by violence or to suppress another group because of its religious beliefs or practices. The Muslim conquests, the French wars of religion, the Crusades, and the Reconquista are frequently cited historical examples. The nine campaigns of the Christian Crusades, from the eleventh to the thirteenth centuries, resulted in a barbarian invasion of the civilized and sophisticated Byzantine Empire and ultimately brought about the ruin of Byzantine civilization. The history of holy war witnessed that religious ideals were besmirched by cruelty and small-mindedness. Those wars were nothing more than a vicious act of intolerance in the name of God.

The wise religionists should want to outdo one another in virtuous acts instead of belligerent attacks on others. Our soul is a recipient of God's wisdom, just like the candlewick that can be lit with light (wisdom) to illuminate the world. Muslims and Christians could do a lot better together if they cooperated with one another to model virtuous acts and respect for one another's beliefs. It is regretful that different religious groups criticize or fight against one another. This became much more serious when displayed by fundamentalists of contemporary religions. No matter what religion one practices, the core virtues that one must put at the forefront today for world order are compassion, humanism, and tolerance. The gospels say that true Christian compassion should extend to all, even to the extent of loving one's enemies. In the Islamic tradition, foremost among God's attributes are mercy and compassion, and he guides humanity to the right way. Islam teaches that God, as referenced in the Koran, is the only God, but it should be recognized that the same God is worshiped by members of other Abrahamic religions, namely, Christianity and Judaism.

According to Buddha, compassion makes the heart of the good move at the pain of others. It crushes and destroys the pain of others. It is called compassion because it shelters and embraces the distressed. In Hindu traditions, compassion is called *daya*, and along with charity and self-control, it is one of the three central virtues. In fact, humans have the ability to conjure up the feeling of compassion toward others with or without religion. "Religion" is a modern concept that suggests a particular spiritual practice and worship. Thus, it is not a universal feature of all cultures but rather a particular idea that first developed in Europe under the influence of Christianity. Let's not forget that the human world is full of good people who don't want to be a part of any religious belief systems yet who are using their free will to perform good deeds in compassion. Thus, true compassion transcends borders, boundaries, economies, color, religion, and politics. Action of compassion speaks louder than religious bigotry. As Meister Eckhart (1260–1327) described, "You may call God love, you may call God goodness. But the best name for God is compassion."[25]

Compassion is the highest quality of human emotion produced out of the limbic system of the brain, bound by the cingulate gyrus belt that coordinates sensory input with emotions. Most human behaviors are triggered by this limbic region. The limbic system (figure 6), located just beneath the cerebrum on both sides of the thalamus, is not only responsible for our emotional lives but also many higher mental functions, such as learning and formation of memory.

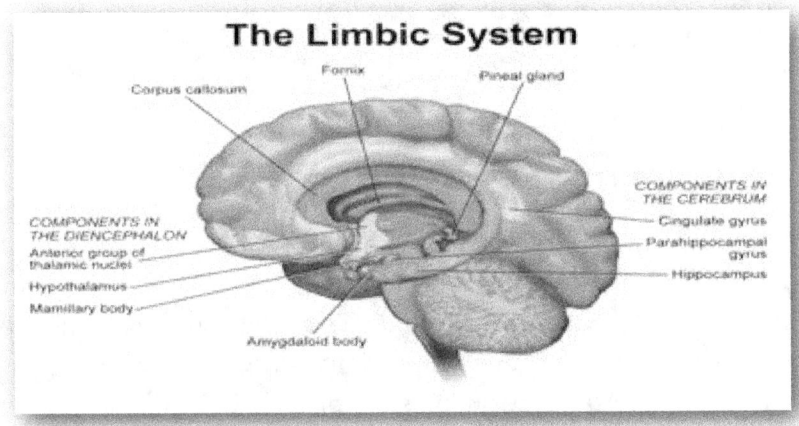

Figure 6: Limbic system
(Source: https://en.wikipedia.org.)

The mind waves hover around this emotional region. Not knowing how to break through the barrier to reach out to the higher region of the brain (the frontal lobes), the mind wave can become tangled in an emotional world that

---

25 *Meister Eckhart: Sermons and Treatises*, Vol. 2, trans. O. C. Walshe, (Watkins Publishing, London, 1981).

can be quite chaotic, sometimes far away from true happiness. Our mind can be compared to crude fossil fuels that can be refined by the soul. With this analogy, compassion is the most refined human emotion that can transcend self-centeredness toward the frontal lobe (figure 7) where rationality is accessible. The frontal lobe is quite unique in the human brain; no other mammals possess it. Once our refined mind reaches the frontal lobe, it can expand into the ethereal world, transcending smallness—an ephemerality of our existence on Earth, reaching out to the realm of universality.

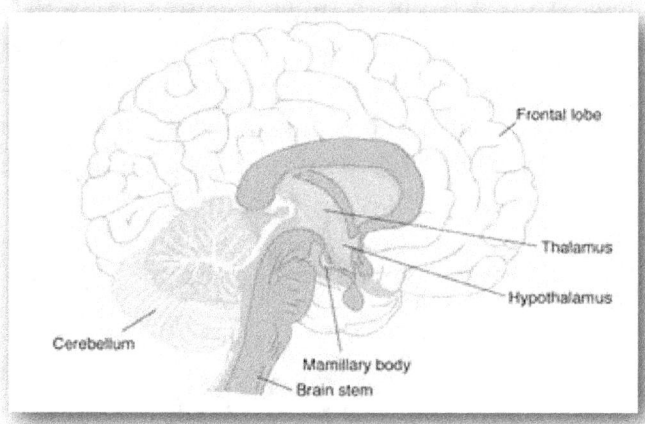

Figure 7: Frontal lobe
(Source: https://en.wikipedia.org.)

The function of the **frontal lobe** involves the ability to project future consequences resulting from current actions: the choice between good and bad actions, the override and suppression of socially unacceptable responses, and the determination of similarities and differences between things or events. The frontal lobe also plays an important part in retaining longer-term memories that are not task based. These are often memories associated with emotions derived from input from the limbic midbrain. The frontal lobe modifies those emotions to generally fit socially acceptable norms.

According to Buddhism, the best part of the invisible world is called "nirvana," or "liberation," which can be reached by compassion, our best emotion. Our mind comprises invisible particle waves that create many visible things.

Going back to the emotional region of our brain, there is scientific speculation that the thalamus creates gamma waves, the fastest frequency of our brain wave during meditation. The thalamus, situated between the frontal lobe and the midbrain (whose functions are the relaying of sensory and motor signals to the cerebral cortex and the regulation of consciousness, sleep, and alertness) may be the fountain of soul. It is noted that humans are not the sole possessors of the core thalamic brain. We share it with all mammals, going back to the earliest ones some two hundred million years ago. That is not to say that all mammals have higher-level consciousness. Other mammals share our sensorimotor cortex and thalamus but have quite smaller frontal lobes to transcend limbic activities. The gamma wave seems to me the bridge between our brain world and the cosmic universe. This wave originates in the thalamus and moves from the back of the brain to the front and back again forty times per second. The neuroscientists believe that gamma waves are able to link information from all parts of the brain; thus the entire brain is influenced by the gamma wave. Something remarkable happened when the Tibetan monks were asked to focus on feelings of compassion: their brain almost immediately went into the gamma frequency in a very rhythmic and coherent pattern. Experiments on Tibetan Buddhist monks have shown a correlation between transcendental mental states and gamma waves. Human compassion is the most refined emotion that can sublimate many other raw emotions, such as desire, sadness, anger, fear, and so on and so forth in meditation. When these emotions are purified to bring about spiritual renewal or release from tension, we may call it catharsis.

If we call the motions of brain waves "mind," the mind can be refined or stay chaotic depending on the strength of soul. The soul, in many religious, philosophical, and mythological traditions, is the immortal essence of a living thing. According to the Abrahamic religions in most of their forms, souls—or at least immortal souls—belong only to human beings. If the waves of the brain produce our mind, the soul moves in the fastest frequency discovered as gamma waves with a frequency range of 40–100 Hz. In other words, our soul belongs to the cosmic universe, and through this wave, we receive infallible wisdom and knowledge from the invisible cosmic world. The religions' beliefs in the corporeal world seem to be nothing but a voice of souls that are gravitated toward the core spirit of the universe, source of order in the universe. This divine spirit has a special mystic influence upon the human soul, illuminating it and nourishing it with a higher spiritual food of which the smallest piece has the same vitality as the whole. The idea of Divine Master, or Creator of all things, has been acknowledged and propagated throughout the world with no scientific evidence of God for several millennia. But as our frontal brain has expanded rapidly in the short human history of evolution, these ideas of religion have gone through a series of evolutionary processes. With more scientific information of the modern earthly world, we can refine the original ideas of religion in light of new knowledge, leaving God's presence unchanged—as His spirit is infinite, omnipresent, omniscient, and omnipotent. It is clear to me, then, we can reach God's spirit in our brain through gamma waves. In fact, our brain is a miniature universe operating in a similar way to how the cosmic universe operates. We may want to remember Jesus's quote: "The Kingdom of God is within you." The true spirit of the kingdom is compassion. Here's another quote by Buddha: "All that we are is the result of what we have thought. The mind is everything what we think we become." That is, we can refine our mind by dwelling in the idea of compassion.

SOUL AND COMPASSION

I consider compassion the core human value that must be embedded in the justice system of modern democratic societies. The Dalai Lama once said, "Compassion is a necessity, not a luxury," and that without it humanity cannot survive. Compassion is like a *gluon*, defined in quantum physics as the so-called messenger particle of the strong nuclear force, which binds subatomic particles known as "quarks." Or compassion is like electromagnetic force, the main glue that holds molecules together. In other words, compassion is the binding force in human society that perpetuates human civilization in harmony. Compassion is a process of connecting with one another, of identifying with another person. This identification with others through compassion can lead to increased motivation to do something in an effort to relieve the suffering of others. It is the emotion one feels in response to the suffering of others that motivates a desire to help. The Dalai Lama wrote, "According to Buddhism, compassion is an aspiration, a state of mind, wanting others to be free from suffering. It's not passive—it's not empathy alone—but rather an empathetic altruism that actively strives to free others from suffering. Genuine compassion must have both wisdom and loving-kindness. That is to say, one must understand the nature of the suffering from which we wish to free others (this is wisdom), and one must experience deep intimacy and empathy with other sentient beings. This is loving-kindness."

In a 2009 small fMRI experiment, Mary Helen Immordino-Yang and colleagues at the Brain and Creativity Institute studied strong feelings of compassion for social and physical pain in others. Both feelings involved an expected change in activity in the anterior insula, anterior cingulate, hypo-thalamus, and midbrain, but the researchers also found a previously unde-scribed pattern of cortical activity on the posterior medial surface of each brain hemisphere—a region involved in the default mode of brain function and implicated in self-related processes. Compassion for social pain in oth-ers was associated with strong activation in the interoceptive, inferior/pos-terior portion of this region, while compassion for physical pain in others involved heightened activity in the exteroceptive, superior/anterior portion. Activity in the anterior insula related to compassion for social pain peaked later and endured longer than that associated with compassion for physical pain. Compassionate emotions in relation to others have effects on the pre-frontal cortex, inferior frontal cortex, and the midbrain. Feelings and acts of compassion have been found to simulate areas known to regulate homeostasis, such as the insular cortex and hypothalamus.

Compassion is the most refined human emotion close to God's core spirit, and when based on cerebral notions such as fairness, justice, and interdepen-dence, it is considered rational in nature and its application understood as an activity based on sound judgment. There is also an aspect of compassion that regards a quantitative dimension such that an individual's compassion is often given a property of depth, vigor, or passion. That is to say, compassion is not just a passive feeling; it relates to the frontal brain and a call to take action to alleviate the pain of others. The etymology of compassion is Latin, meaning cosuffering. More involved than simple empathy, compassion commonly gives rise to an active desire to alleviate another's suffering.

The whole purpose of religion is to refine our minds with ideas of compassion, patience, tolerance, humility, and forgiveness. That is, we want to build a noble character in our brain waves with God's wisdom. The greatest degree of inner tranquility comes from development of such noble qualities. The more we care for the well-being of others, the greater our own sense of well-being. Cultivating close, warmhearted feelings for others evokes peaceful feelings within our soul. This helps remove whatever fears or tension recipients may experience and gives them the strength to cope with any obstacles they face with a grateful attitude—because compassion is the bridge between our souls, connecting us with keen awareness of the interdependence of all living beings. That is, we are part of all, and all involve in one another within the circle of God's kingdom, as Meister Eckhart (1260–1328) said, "What God gives is His being, and His being is His goodness, and His goodness is His love (compassion)."

Chapter 4

DIVINE QUALITY IN HUMANITY

NOBLE CHARACTER BUILDING THROUGH COMPASSION

The divine quality of humankind is not an innate attribute but a materialization of spiritual maturity developed out of the seed of goodness. Goodness is defined as God's love according to Christianity, and the love here refers to the fatherly love of God for humankind. The best way humans can express reciprocal love for God is by spreading God's goodness to others in interactions with fellow men and women—desiring and acting in the best interests of others. Love being a heavenly principle commanded by God, must be obeyed if humankind desires joint happiness and peace on Earth. God's love, full of goodness, is infused into human souls to inspire them to do good things for others without being asked.

The love energy—I prefer to call it "compassion"—no doubt is the foundation of noble character. An admirable character is not inherited from genetics or learned in schools. Noble character doesn't come from humankind's high intelligence or its intellectual background alone. It's built steadily over time through self-discipline, nurtured by the universal wisdom of God. If actions and deeds are the actualization of our invisible mind, our mind is directed by character built in our soul that seems to be the buttress at the center of brain, inside of the limbic midbrain, guiding our mind waves. Building good character is an ongoing exercise for one's spiritual growth and development that involves seeking daily wisdom—the nourishment that builds noble character. People feel deep warmth and comfort when they deal with a person of noble character. The goodness expressed by noble character is heavenly music enshrined in compassion. People trust a man or woman of noble character because he or she shines with compassion for his fellow humans. He or she has no greed, resentment, anger, fear, judgment, or cynicism. He or she is humble, content, self-confident, broad minded, understanding, tolerant, and peace loving. A person of noble character is an enlightened human soul who understands the nature of salvation.

HUMILITY MODELED BY CHRIST

The nature of salvation can be best explained by Christianity as God's magnanimous forgiveness of human ignorance, enabling reconciliation between His creation and Himself. When a human soul awakens to believe in God's existence and his grand magnanimity, the person has risen from his or her ignorance to become partakers of the divine nature comfortably, having been reconciled to God. Thus, it can be said that Jesus Christ was the bridge between the human world and invisible world that has an abundance of resources for human happiness. Christ was on Earth to accomplish his grand mission of teaching mortals how to build the kingdom of heaven on Earth with humanism and humility. In order to achieve peace and harmony on Earth, he urged humankind to depend on none other than God for his perfect knowledge and wisdom: "Thou shalt love God with all thy heart and with all thy soul, and with all thy mind." This is the first commandment delivered by Christ. And the second is the propagation of love in the visible world: "Thou shalt love thy fellow man as thyself." On these two commandments hang all the laws and human morality, for these are the core universal principles reflecting the grace of God and his harmonic law.

Christ showed compassion for the poor, commanding humans to develop the divine quality of humankind by caring for and helping one another. He instilled in the human mind the conceptual possibility and hope of an earthly kingdom if humankind just followed his commandments. Simply, the purpose of his commandments is none other than to make all human beings pursue happiness via God's compassion. Christ encouraged earthlings to continue seeking heavenly knowledge through scientific endeavor and wisdom to practice human virtue. The virtuous spirit is a humble spirit that nurtures noble character in the soul. Although the ideas of humility have been emphasized in all major religions of the human world, it was Christ who first brought humility to light by singling it out as the most important of all virtues. Some thoughtful definitions of "humility" described by many religious leaders and philosophers following in Christ's footsteps are modest behavior, selflessness, and the giving of respect. More precisely, it's an acknowledgment of imperfection of self and tolerance toward people you disagree with, and it's the courage necessary to undertake tasks that are difficult, tedious, or unglamorous, and to graciously accept the sacrifices involved. Humility also is referred to as the condition or quality of being meager and humble in living yet demonstrating gratitude. A good historical example of this is the American pilgrimage and first Thanksgiving. Humility gives power to endure despair and the ability to confront crisis, uncertainty, or intimidation without fear. Humility is a mature mental attitude and action in relationship with God and our fellow humans in society. Christ, who is the ultimate definition of humility himself, prioritizes the eight beatitudes by highlighting humility in two different ways at the very top of the list: "Blessed are the poor in spirit, for theirs is the kingdom of heaven; Blessed are the meek, for they shall inherit the earth."[26] He was implying that only those humble in spirit can become the chalice that receives God's grace. Humility seems to evoke cosmic sympathy in a powerful

---

26 The eight beatitudes of Jesus: "Blessed are the poor in spirit, for theirs is the kingdom of heaven; Blessed are they who mourn, for they shall be comforted; Blessed are the meek, for they shall inherit the earth; Blessed are they who hunger and thirst for righteousness, for they shall be satisfied; Blessed are the merciful, for they shall obtain mercy; Blessed are the pure of heart, for they shall see God; Blessed are the peacemakers, for they shall be called children of God; and Blessed are they who are persecuted for the sake of righteousness, for theirs is the kingdom of heaven" (Matthew 5:3–10).

way. It seems that God's most cherished spirit is a humble soul upon which noble character is built. When a man is seeking cosmic knowledge in humility, he can receive it on the wings of wisdom. To put it differently, humility is like good fertile land, where good crops of goodness can grow and multiply. Christ, through parables, taught humans to be content in the lowest place with no honor or reward.

This may be very difficult for the ordinary mind to practice, for human nature generally wants instant reward and honor when doing something worthwhile. The harmonic law of the universe commands humans to learn and practice humility in relationship with their fellow human beings within the sphere of humanism. The opposite end of humility is pride, the sense of having a high opinion of oneself. Pride is often described as vanity, vainglory, arrogance, greed, or selfishness, along with an ungrateful attitude, which adds little value to humanism in interactions. It stands as an undesirable human trait, damaging tremendously, not only the interactions among humankind but also the survival of the self, due to the fact that human survival depends on interconnectedness with fellow humans. Martial arts master Bruce Lee described pride in his analogy: "Notice that the stiffest tree is most easily cracked, while the bamboo or willow survives by bending with the wind." Humility provides a human with a lot more freedom and flexibility than pride. Humility acknowledges that all powers and abilities are not lodged in oneself and that every soul in this world is related in kinship, no matter how low its light burns.

Looking up the clear night sky and observing the unfathomable expanse of the universe containing a countless number of galaxies, luminous stars, and planets evenly scattered throughout the infinite space, as humans we can begin to wonder and hope that behind these facts of mass, distance, and time, there is a universal law of cosmic order by design. It may be difficult to understand why all the particles in an infinite space should be so accurately poised, as if they stand still in a perfect equilibrium. We can conclude that harmony in the cosmic system is the effect of choice rather than of random display. Such wonderment and awe certainly enjoins us with humility, with the feeling that we human beings are indeed small living creatures on Earth—one of the billions of planets in the visible universe. It goes without saying that however small we may be, we humans are ideational mammals, quite different from other species in conceptualizing and behaving. We humans are capable of making behavioral choices that may bring a better or the best outcome for human happiness and survival.

To fathom how vast the universe is, who the Master of the universe is, what our life's purpose is, and how everyone inhales the same air in no more than equal amount to survive...these sorts of questions can put us in the direction of humility, to accepting the truth of universal harmony. One does not have to be a religionist to admire the beauty of the logical simplicity of the harmonic order, which we can grasp humbly. Once Albert Einstein (1879–1955) expressed his religious view by saying, "Scientific research can reduce superstition by encouraging people to think and view things in terms of cause and effect. Certain it is that a conviction, akin to religious feeling, of the rationality and intelligibility of the world lies behind all scientific work of a higher order. This firm belief, a belief bound up with a deep feeling, in a superior mind that reveals itself in the world of experience, represents my conception of God."[27] Such a broad pantheistic concept of deity is much more palatable and defendable than strict religionistic dogmas when we are discussing the universal truth reachable by scientific endeavors in the modern world. Truth is sometimes as strange as fiction and takes a long time to reveal itself for universal acceptance. But the path toward the truth is safe and steady if we make the choice of virtue and have faith in the infinite spirit of the Master for His harmonic law. The quality of faith is an active state of mind, different from mere belief. It is the reverence to the Cosmic Master Spirit of omniscience, omnipresence, and omnipotence and behaving in accordance to His commands involving intellect, humility, and will.

The infinite variety of human knowledge is like the infinite number of melodies produced from a single instrument of truth. God is the owner of that instrument, and this truth is delivered through the voice of Christ. Indeed, people who are familiar with the golden ratio (Φ) will be able to understand what Christ is talking about. In one of his parables, Christ used the mustard

---

27 Albert Einstein, *On Scientific Truth*, Essay (National Academy of Sciences, 1980).

seed as a model of the earthly kingdom. The seed of harmony is compassion, which grows to cover the entire world, spreading peaceful humanism so that even nonbelievers can be drawn to it. Human spiritual maturity begins with humility to develop noble character in the soul. Humility is the quality of being modest and respectful. Humility is described by Christian theology as "quality by which a person, considering his own defects, has a humble opinion of himself and willingly submits himself to God and to others for God's sake."[28] Humility manifests itself through attitudes and actions in relationship with divinity and our fellow humans on Earth. The harmonic law of the universe commands humans to learn and practice humility in relationships with their fellow human beings. The discussion of God's commandment for humility will be continued in the ensuing chapters in terms of civic virtue, for humility should be applied as the core civic virtue to enhance effectiveness in government leadership.

A divine quality such as humility empowers others and makes others feel respected and important. When we are full of pride, we are self-focused, and when we are self-focused, we can't see others' needs, and we can't see God. We are not here on Earth to indulge in powerful positions by hoarding wealth or justifying brutal competitions. We're here to serve one another and to bring peace and beauty to Earth by obeying the cosmic law—harmony. Human-group life is like water molecules that have strong hydrogen bonding. Just as hydrogen bonding explains the physical characteristics of water, our human life on Earth is bound by harmonic law and divine grace. In many ways, human life flows like water and evaporates when the time comes, withdrawn from corporeality into the invisible cosmos. Until then, we individually and collectively are responsible for our proper roles in the given society with the virtue of humility to accord with the harmonic law of the universe.

HUMANISM AS VIRTUE OF SOCIETY

When Saint Paul said, "We who are strong ought to bear with the failings of the weak and not to please ourselves; let each of us please our fellowmen

---

28 Humility: from The Catholic Encyclopedia (Robert Appleton Company, 1920)

for the good, for building up," he was underscoring the humanistic morality based on relational ethics of caring and helping one another as taught by
Christ. This is a basic principle of humanism. Christ is depicted as a three-
dimensional form of God's spirit, just as the Great Pyramid is an embodiment
of harmonic law, sent to Earth to reiterate and emphasize, verbally in human
language, the criticality of harmony in the world. He reminded us of the
golden ratio, of divine proportion, by saying, "The Father's kingdom is spread
out upon the earth, and people don't see it" (Thomas 113[29]). Likewise, he
reminded earthlings that the divine proportion—harmonic law—is a fundamental law of heaven: "The kingdom of heaven is like a mustard seed, which
a man took and planted in his field. Though it is the smallest of all your seeds,
yet when it grows, it is the largest of garden plants and becomes a tree, so that
the birds of the air come and perch in its branches" (Matt. 13:31).

---

29 The Gospel according to Thomas is an early Christian noncanonical sayings-gospel that many
scholars believe provides insight into the oral gospel traditions. it is difficult to date Thomas but
most interpreters place its writing in the second century. It does not tell the story of the life and
death of Jesus but offers the reader his teachings about the kingdom of God.

Chapter 5

ROLE OF GOVERNMENT IN CIVIL SOCIETY

COLLECTIVE MISSION OF MANKIND

The collective mission of humankind is to preserve the beauty and harmony on Earth. That is to say our mission is conscious commitment devoted to beauty and harmony as our life's dream. Think of the right triangle. The vertical line represents our faith in God, responding to God's compassion on us and the horizontal line our mission of compassion to others. When the mission is noble and inspiring, it gives dignity and pleasure to its participants, and thus shared common purpose provides the noble energy for collective effort. And when the purpose promises a better life, it gives hope to all. On an individual level, not all of us can do great things as mission workers on Earth, but it counts big when we do small things with great love in humble spirit as long as human happiness is the bedrock of our purpose. There's nothing that pleases God more than humility. Acknowledging that God is our true Creator and that He alone can be glorified for all good things we do on Earth helps us to build a noble character within our soul. In the end, the sum of individual noble characters builds a kingdom on Earth with a shared sense of mission; binding an individual's mission with the group mission is just like water molecules holding on to one another via hydrogen bonds to form a vast ocean.

A civil society has two components—government and citizens—working together in a noble mission to achieve human happiness. Let's not forget that the end of civil society is human happiness. The best government equates to the best way of life for all citizens of a given society. Since the best way of life is living nobly and according to virtue, the best government is the one that promotes this life. No doubt, then, our collective mission—combining government and citizens—is none other than noble duty to achieve happiness for all, with the hope to perpetuate and maintain the civil society.

A civil society can be formed on the foundation of a democratic-republican principle, which contains the will of people and rule of justice established by law that is the responsibility of government. Since a majority of the common people are not capable of being lawmakers, they elect better, more suitable representatives to make up the body of government, entrusting them with the promulgation of laws for them in an articulate and unambiguous manner to represent their common will of good. Thus, a government, with such a noble duty, is a leader of the people in defining the nature of the common good and civil liberty to which all people are willing to agree by general will. To ensure the happiness of citizens, lawmakers must allow flexibility in constitutional promulgation or any other policy matters in expectation of the challenges intrinsic to the evolutionary nature of society, with constant vigilance to the common goods for all under the binding principle of civil society between government and citizens. That is to say, citizens and government are bound by the same grand mission to achieve the same goal under the most sublime command of God upon which our purpose in life is dependent.

In discussion of role of government in reflection of Phi – harmonic law of universe - perhaps it is reasonable to pick one country, namely America, to examine how its government operates comparing with other advanced democratic nations of the world today. America, quite larger than most advanced Western nations geographically, has been dazzling the world for some time with quick blooming economic and military power.   But sadly, many Americans don't know much about their government today and are unable to name their representatives in Congress or even key figures in their local governments. For some people, the government doesn't seem to play a major role in their lives, so they do not pay much attention to politics. Others complain about the difficulty involved in learning about the issues and their representatives, even at a state and local level. And those who pay attention to congressional actions feel that the government only listens to special-interest groups, not to average citizens who wish to see their government do something for them in a tangible way.

Citizens unequivocally like to feel included and respected as valuable citizens of the society and nation. In reality the majority of citizens in the United States continues to distrust the media and perceive the news as biased and thus don't trust what they see on television or read in the newspapers. Americans' trust in mass media has generally been edging downward from high levels in the late 1990s or early 2000s. Political cynicism has become common, and Americans no longer believe in the government's ability for effective change. The wide strain of criticism is that the federal government's priorities are misplaced and that government policies unfairly benefit moneyed groups while not doing enough to help average Americans. In recent years the annual surveys conducted by Gallup poll show quite poor ratings of Congress's job performance, and at the same time, the disapproval rate has gone up to over 80 percent. The disapproval rate for Congress seems to keep increasing as time goes on. Americans' trust in each of the three branches of the federal government was at or near the lowest in Gallup's trends as of September 2014 (dating back to the early 1970s) as well.

GOVERNMENT'S ROLE DEFINED BY JAMES MADISON AND JOHN LOCKE

James Madison (1751–1836), the fourth US president and one of America's founding fathers, drew his most fundamental principles of liberty and government from John Locke's political view documented in *Two Treatises of Government*, with the principal idea being that people, not rulers, are sovereign. Madison defined the role of government as follows: "The great desideratum (necessity) in Government is to modify the sovereignty so that it may be sufficiently neutral between different parts of the society to control one part from invading the rights of another."[30]

For Madison, virtue was always the foundation of government, endowed with a higher sanction than the mere will of the majority. To him, the goal of the government is to secure the God-given rights of citizens—that is, government exists simply to secure the rights that God has endowed us. According to Madison, the government's sole function is the protection of those rights via the powers given in the Constitution. He was the first president to have served in the US Congress, and he was a leader in the first US Congress, drafting many basic laws and was responsible for the first ten amendments to the Constitution; thus, he is also known as the father of the Bill of Rights. All powers assigned to the government are a representation of the people's will and ultimately held by the people. That is to say, no original, organic, or self-possessed powers existed in the government without its people. As stated above, Madison was very much influenced by John Locke's political philosophy. John Locke (1632–1704) was a British philosopher who was especially influential on American politics in its beginning stage. His writings influenced Voltaire, Rousseau, and many Scottish Enlightenment thinkers, as well as the American revolutionaries. Locke's contributions to classical republicanism and liberal theory are reflected in the American Declaration of Independence. He expressed the view that government is morally obligated to serve people, namely, by protecting life, liberty, and property.

Locke believed that the proper role of government should allow humans to flourish as individuals and as societies, both materially and spiritually. Locke considered moral duty, with a set of laws specific to humanity in accordance with God's will, to be the foundation in determining the proper role of government. This emphasizes that government legislations (sets of laws) must be based on morality dictated by reason (law of nature) and the law of God, where the laws of nature shouldn't contradict the law of God—otherwise, they are ill made. Locke assumed, without question, supremacy of God's law beyond the law of nature or reasoning power when he said: "There is an eternal, most powerful, and most knowing Being which whether any one will

---

30 James Madison, *Letter to Thomas Jefferson* (October 24, 1787).

please to call God, it matters not. Eternal God alone can produce thinking, perceiving beings, such as we find ourselves to be."[31] Locke states that God gave us our capacity for reason to aid us in the search for truth, or God's will. Therefore, we can reason that, since we are all equally God's children, He must want everyone to be happy. If one person makes another unhappy by causing him or her pain, that person has rejected God's will. Therefore, each person has a duty to preserve other people as well as himself or herself.

If we all must come to discover the truth through reason, then no one man (or woman) is better able to discover truth than any other man. For this reason, political leaders cannot impose their beliefs to fool people. Locke insists that if men or women were to follow the government blindly, they would be surrendering their own reason and truth, thus violating God's law. There is no dispute that John Locke greatly influenced the American founding principles, with the founding fathers seeking to position themselves as Enlightenment thinkers in the age of reason, although they did not incorporate Locke's core idea of public good in the constitutional theme.

ADAM SMITH'S FREE-MARKET THEORY

In addition to John Locke's philosophy, the founding fathers adopted the free-market economic principles of Adam Smith, who believed that there is an invisible hand guiding the economic prosperity of society. Adam Smith (1723–90), a Scottish social philosopher and political economist, proposed a theory that in a free and unregulated market, where anybody can become a producer or a consumer, people's demand of goods and their production of the same goods will be equal, and the allocation of their resources for production and consumption of different goods will be optimal for the welfare of the society. Put it another way, Smith suggested that the invisible hand of the market forces of demand and supply will achieve the most efficient level of production, consumption, and distribution of goods in the society without government intervention. The idea of an invisible hand guiding the market for the best social outcome created a very strong argument in favor of free

---

31 John Locke, "An Essay Concerning Human Understanding," Book IV, Chapter 10, in *Of Our Knowledge of the Existence of a God* (Prometheus Books, 1995).

markets and has been the standard argument against governments controlling production or consumption in any form that interferes with that free market.

The assumptions supporting Adam Smith's "invisible hand" theory of market economy were probably reasonable for America two hundred years ago. Businesses were mostly small, individual proprietorships, none of which individually could measurably affect prices or quantities in their markets as a whole. Transactions were mostly face to face and personal, between producer and consumer, which left little room for deception or misinformation. During Smith's time, the human population was too small to inflict any irreversible damage to the natural environment, and strong moral and social values clearly defined the bounds of acceptable behavior. Under these conditions, the "invisible hand" was indeed a protector of the general economic welfare. However, Adam Smith emphasized that the government should be held responsible for defense of the society above all, protecting members of society from the injustice or oppression of other members while suggesting freedom of enterprise and property rights. Smith decisively had a critical view on property, saying, "Wherever there is great property, there is great inequality...Civil government, so far as it is instituted for the security of property, is in reality instituted for the defense of the rich against the poor, or of those who have some property against those who have none at all."[32]

The great inequality is here today in America just as Adam Smith predicted! Modern capitalism traces its roots to Adam Smith and his book, *Wealth of Nations*, which has served, perhaps more than any other economic work, as a guide to the formulation of the economic policies of America. His vision of the uncomplicated role of government, nevertheless, has grown beyond the bounds of those simple duties that were suitable during his time, as the role of government in the United States and other Western democracies has expanded dramatically over the past century. Compared to its pre-twentieth-century functions, today's government has to take on new and vast roles not only to prevent the injustice of great inequality (as Adam Smith warned) but also to implement a host of other programs that typically compose a modern welfare state.

---

32 Adam Smith, *Wealth of Nations*, Book V, Chapter I, Part II: On the Expense of Justice (University of Chicago Press, 1977).

SOCIAL DEMOCRACY OF WELFARE STATE

The welfare state usually refers to an ideal model wherein the government accepts responsibility for the provision of comprehensive and universal welfare for its citizens. The concept of welfare state is predominantly a European evolution in socioeconomic and political reasoning, combining Plato-Aristotelian ideas of "good society" and Christian humanism. The misconception of welfare state—that it undermines productivity, efficiency, and economic growth—must be corrected with the opposite fact: that welfare-state programs complement capitalism and increase productivity, efficiency, and economic growth. The welfare state is not the antithesis of a capitalistic nation. In fact, many wealthy nations today are welfare states—that is, they are primarily capitalist states with large, selective doses of socialism, by which the economic insecurity and instability produced by a free-market economy can be substantially reduced. The European welfare state was consolidated in the coherent programs of social-democratic parties, and their most common target areas included education, public health, and guaranteed old-age insurance.

CRITIQUE OF THE US CONSTITUTION

Unfortunately, nothing in the US Constitution would suggest that the general welfare of public would be protected from the forces of economic self-interest as warned by Adam Smith. Hence, the American welfare system lacks a comprehensive structure, with no clear provision stated in the Constitution. The preamble of the Constitution establishes no powers or rights in that regard, and no further development of what "general welfare" means can be traced, based on the mention of it in the Constitution. According to the 1828 edition of Noah Webster's *American Dictionary of the English Language*, the word "welfare" was defined in two different connotations (forty years after it was written in the Constitution) for citizens and government. For individuals, welfare means "exemption from misfortune, sickness, calamity, or evil; the enjoyment of health and the common blessings of life; and prosperity and happiness." For government, it means "exemption from any unusual evil or calamity; the enjoyment of peace and prosperity, or the ordinary blessings of society." A clear distinction is made with respect to welfare as applied to people and government. In the US Constitution, the word "welfare" is used in the context of government and not people. The welfare of the United States is not congruent with the welfare of individuals, people, or citizens.

Interestingly, the US Constitution is older than any of the European constitutions, while the history of the United States is much younger than any of the European countries. There have been many proposals for substantial change to the US Constitution but with no tangible progress. Therefore, today we still have a two-hundred-year-old Constitution in America. Thomas Jefferson (1743–1826) himself was wary of the power of the dead over the living in the form of an unchanging Constitution. Thomas Jefferson wisely warned rigid conservatives: "Some men look at constitutions with sanctimonious reverence, and deem them like the ark of covenant, too sacred to be touched…Laws and institutions must go hand in hand with the progress of the human mind…We might as well require a man to wear still the coat which fitted him when a boy, as civilized societies to remain under the regimen of their barbarous ancestors."[33]

Thomas Jefferson was a draftsman of the Declaration of Independence and the third US president (1801–9).[34] He was also responsible for the Louisiana Purchase. He very likely would have encouraged prudent public policy changes to meet today's dynamic socioeconomic issues of daunting

---

33 Thomas Jefferson, *Letter to Samuel Kercheval* (Monticello, July 12, 1816).

34 Thomas Jefferson is the most legendary president of America, and his legacy still shines as bright as the North Star in the heavens. American myth is created by his immortal words in the Declaration of Independence: "We hold these truths to be self-evident, that all men are created equal, that they are endowed by their Creator with certain unalienable Rights, that among these are Life, Liberty and the pursuit of Happiness.--That to secure these rights, Governments are instituted among Men, deriving their just powers from the consent of the governed…That whenever any Form of Government becomes destructive of these ends, it is the Right of the People to alter or to abolish it, and to institute new Government, laying its Foundation on such Principles, and organizing its Powers in such Form, as to them shall seem most likely to effect their Safety and Happiness. " Jefferson's powerful voice of equal human rights and happiness engraved on the Declaration still resonates throughout the world. Merrill D Peterson, *The Jefferson Image in the American Mind* (Oxford University Press, 1960).

scope. Survival of the fittest wasn't his governmental doctrine, but prudence and virtue with concern for the common man's welfare were Jeffersonian governmental values, not often acknowledged by far-right Republican conservatives. The preamble of the Constitution, summing up the spirit of the Constitution written over two hundred years ago, does not say that the primary role of government is to provide for the general welfare for the people. At best, those writers inserted the words "to promote" instead of clearly saying "to provide." These two terms have quite different meanings; they are not synonyms. In the governmental mission statement, "to provide" means a mandated duty that requires government action, while "to promote" denotes nonmandatory, unobligated solicitation. The founders nevertheless believed that protecting private-property rights was an important key role of the government. It is interesting that the founding fathers picked a Lockean principle of government, in the role of protecting private-property rights but deliberately dismissed Locke's warning on excessive property rights that would create an inequality problem.

The preamble is the guiding principle of the Constitution, with the Constitution being the fundamental law guiding the nation. Thus, it is reliable evidence of the founding fathers' intentions regarding the Constitution's meaning and what they hoped it would achieve. So, the preamble is the nation's mission statement that identifies the "spirit" of the Constitution. It embodied the founders' philosophies, goals, ambitions, and mores. However, nothing in the US Constitution would lead us to believe that the founders intended to develop a civil society by providing welfare for the people and promoting the peace of the world. Such is, of course, a modern concept of civil society.

The world has changed since the preamble was written two hundred years ago. Civil society is where people voluntarily associate themselves with a group to advance common interests and happiness for all, which include world peace as well. Therefore, the government of civil society, representing the collective will of the people, has a noble duty to achieve just that. It is thus unquestionable that the government has to develop a mission statement, in affirmation of the citizens' will, to preserve civil society with the happiness of citizens in mind. Such is the constitutional mission statement.

With an unambiguous mission statement, the government could lead a civil society in where all can work collectively together toward solving problems and meeting society's changing needs with little disagreement. In order to create and preserve a civil society, the government needs to take a strong leadership role in the common good instead of actively protecting the wealthy who are hiving off themselves. Adam Ferguson (1723–1816), a Scottish philosopher known as the father of modern sociology, in *An Essay on the History of Civil Society*, describes the civic virtue of politicians and also describes the political corruption that comes with capitalists' selfish interests, which can destroy civil society:

> The natural disposition of man to humanity, and the warmth of his temper, may raise his character to this fortunate pitch. His elevation, in a great measure, depends on the form of his society; but he can, without incurring the charge of corruption, accommodate himself to great variations in the constitutions of government...When mere riches, or court-favor, are supposed to constitute rank; the mind is misled from the consideration of qualities on which it ought to rely. Magnanimity, courage, and the love of mankind, are sacrificed to avarice and vanity, or suppressed under a sense of dependence. The individual considers his community so far only as it can be rendered subservient to his personal advancement or profit: he states himself in competition with his fellow-creatures; and, urged by the passions of emulation, of fear and jealousy, of envy and malice, he follows the maxims of an animal destined to preserve his separate existence, and to indulge his caprice or his appetite, at the expense of his species... Defects of government, and of law, may be in some cases considered as a symptom of innocence and of virtue. But where power is already established, where the strong are unwilling to suffer restraint, or the weak unable to find a protection, the defects of law are marks of the most perfect corruption.[35]

---

35 Adam Ferguson, "An Essay on the History of Civil Society." Part Sixth, Section 1, *Of Corruption in General*, (Liberty Fund, Online Library of Liberty, 2016).

SIGNIFICANCE OF OCCUPY WALL STREET MOVEMENT

It is clear that today's American democratic-republican government is not endorsing the economic democracy emphasized for civil society. The discontent of citizens is manifested in the recent Occupy Wall Street movement, fighting for civil society and more precisely for the common citizens whose political rights and equal economic opportunities are unprotected. In Lower Manhattan, in a small plaza called Zuccotti Park, the Occupy Wall Street was born in September of 2011. While the first occupiers had originally come to protest Wall Street, once the actual occupation began, however, their game plan was not entirely clear. In spite of this lack of clarity—and also paradoxically because of it—the Occupy movement rapidly began to spread throughout the United States and abroad. From major cities to small towns in rural America, people seemed drawn to this sudden explosion of outrage aimed broadly against all that was wrong with American society. Within two weeks, there were dozens of occupations happening modeled after Zuccotti Park; after a month, there were many hundreds. Every new day saw a whirlwind of developments—new occupations, protests, debates, critiques, and proposed solutions. Though the movement did not issue clear-cut demands, one thing quickly became evident: that this was a movement of the "99 percent," of the broad masses of people robbed of their due share of society's wealth and opportunities by millionaires and billionaires (i.e., by the "1 percent"). The movement aimed to reverse the trend from preceding decades in which the neoliberal agenda of US and global capitalism had shockingly increased social and economic inequality. These citizens are the young men and women who contributed equally to the bounty of economic growth but who are still sinking into poverty, suppressed by the ruthless power of corporate avarice.

It's ironic that American wealth growth is heavily dependent on consumers for national prosperity. But sadly, the bulk of consumers are too poor to accommodate the growth any more. In a true, healthy democratic nation, founded upon the civil society concept, the government is the representation of its citizens' voice. The first duty of the government is to protect its citizens' welfare through equitable wealth distribution, which strengthens the national economy toward long-term prosperity. The enactment and application of appropriate laws to transform the nation into a civil society is not an option but the supreme duty of the government. During the latest deep economic recession (2008–9), the economy shrank in five quarters, including four quarters in a row. It is considered the worst recession since the Depression, with a high unemployment rate coupled with mounting national debt. Yet the excessive compensation for corporate executives and owners did not decrease. This most heinous phenomenon outrages American citizens today.

ALARMING INEQUALITY OF THE US WEALTH DISTRIBUTION

Until the early 1980s, high top-bracket federal income tax rates (91 percent on income over $400, 000 until 1964, then 70 percent on income over $200,000 until 1981[36]) kept huge corporate-executive windfalls off the table. But here's a startling fact: Today after two decades, the nation's top four hundred mega millionaires and billionaires are paying taxes at an effective rate of only 18 percent, when these earners are expected to pay at least at a rate of 35 percent, the same as the corporate rate.

In the meantime, the ratio of CEO pay to the average worker pay in the United States went up to 354:1, according to the report produced by a research team of Harvard Business School, while other advanced countries show a moderate ratio of CEO pay to average worker pay in 2012[37] as shown in table 1.

---

36 Tax Foundation, *Federal Individual Income Tax Rates History, Income Years 1913–2013.*
37 Gretchen Gavett, "CEOs Get Paid Too Much, According to Pretty Much Everyone in the World," *Harvard Business Review*, September 23, 2014.

WHAT AVERAGE WORKERS SHOULD BE PAID
According to each country's ideal CEO-to-worker compensation ratios.

	RATIO		AVERAGE COMPENSATION		
	Actual	*Ideal*	CEO	Worker	*Worker at the ideal ratio*
Australia	93	8.3	$4,183,419	$44,983	$502,012
Austria	36	5.0	1,567,908	43,555	313,582
Czech Republic	110	4.2	2,159,300	19,630	518,229
Denmark	48	2.0	2,186,880	45,560	1,093,440
France	104	6.7	3,965,312	38,132	594,794
Germany	147	6.3	5,912,781	40,223	946,045
Israel	76	3.6	2,189,104	28,804	601,998
Japan	67	6.0	2,354,581	35,143	392,430
Norway	58	2.3	2,551,420	43,990	1,093,481
Poland	28	5.0	561,932	20,069	112,386
Portugal	53	5.0	1,205,326	22,742	241,065
Spain	127	3.0	4,399,915	34,387	1,466,638
Sweden	89	2.2	3,358,326	37,734	1,511,262
Switzerland	148	5.0	7,435,816	50,242	1,487,163
United Kingdom	84	5.3	3,758,412	44,743	704,707
United States	354	6.7	12,259,894	34,645	1,838,975

SOURCE SORAPOP KIATPONGSAN AND MICHAEL I. NORTON, "HOW MUCH (MORE) SHOULD CEOS MAKE?";
AFL- CIO, "CEO-TO-WORKER PAY RATIOS AROUND THE WORLD."   HBR.ORG

Table 1: CEO-to-worker compensation ratios
Source: Harvard Business Revew, September 23, 2014

As the report indicated, the bigger problem by far is executive pay has continued to rise at an enormous rate while the average worker's real wages have been stagnant since the 1970s. Indisputably, only the government can, by forceful means, discourage ruthless wealth hoardings that upset civil society. The top fifty companies have cut 531,000 jobs between November 2008 and April 2010, accounting for three-quarters of layoffs at the five hundred biggest US companies. Topping the list is former Schering-Plough chief Fred Hassan, who took home $49.7 million after selling the drugmaker to Merck in a deal that led to sixteen thousand job cuts. Another CEO whose leadership has come under scrutiny lately is William Weldon of Johnson & Johnson. Weldon took home $25.6 million while firing eighty-nine hundred workers. CEOs are clearly not hurting, but they are causing national poverty by cutting jobs. The problem of executive compensation was seriously addressed at the G20 Summit in 2009 in connection with the economic crisis. It emphasized the need for moral pressure, which national governments should impose on the industries.

There is no question that the government must pay serious attention to unequal distribution of wealth and income, which inevitably breeds public discontent, depression, and anger. The sum of these negative reactions eventually can lead to civic violence. In this regard, true defense, whether it is individual or national, lies in guarding against evildoers who cause the destruction of civil society. It is imperative for the government to recognize that we have an exploitative class structure in America and to understand that the accelerating gap of economic inequality signifies political disconnection from its citizens, which is dangerous to the nation's solidarity and prosperity. More than 40 percent of America's 308 million people are near poverty and disconnected from what is going on with the nation's politics. Such political disconnection is more dangerous to national defense than foreign enemies. Sadly, ordinary citizens do not know how to challenge the mammoth government system to claim their equal rights. They are subjected to too many confusing messages from the mainstream media, and they are unable to articulate their dismal situations for fear of being rebuked or arrested. Such fear keeps poor Americans from challenging the unfair advantages of the rich and from demanding an equitable portion of the nation's wealth. Poor folks (whites, blacks, and Hispanics) suffer from discrimination but do not protest it because they lack the sufficient education to absorb political information adequately. At best they perceive no options other than seeking spiritual comfort from religious salvation or racial solidarity.

A dominant belief of the US Congress today is still free-market capitalism, along with trickle-down economic theories that foster maximum freedom to large corporations and a rich minority. Republican policy makers predominantly believe that the growth of the US economy is dependent on rich enterprises, even though in reality the growth itself does not provide general welfare for the people or sustainable peace for the nation. We can hope that the current disenchantment of citizens with their government will instill Congress with a strong sensibility for the consensus-building process: a consensus concerning basic principles for the happiness of citizens and the proper role of government, which can safeguard civil society.

Chapter 6

CIVIC VIRTUE OF GOVERNMENT

The character traits that constitute civic virtue have been a major discussion of political philosophy for a long time since the days of Plato and Aristotle. Most discussions of civic virtue center around the obligation of citizens to participate in society by performing the minimally necessary activities in support of the state, such as paying taxes. This clearly indicates that an individual person's well-being is not solely attributable to his or her own talents but is a result of societal cooperation. To promote such societal cooperation, civic virtue then involves citizens taking part in ruling and being ruled. This means the required civic virtue applies to both citizens and government. It in turn depends on the kind of political order a society as a sum of citizens aspires to create. To illustrate the common understandings of civic virtue, it is useful to compare two dominant political ideas: liberalism and republicanism in America.

CORNERSTONE OF LIBERALISM

Liberalism is the belief in the importance of liberty and equal rights. It's the philosophy of Enlightenment intellectuals, during eighteenth-century Europe (known as the Age of Enlightenment), who believed that human affairs should be guided by reason and the principles of liberty and equality. They argued that all people are created equal, and therefore, political authority cannot be justified on the basis of "noble blood," privileged connection to God, or any other characteristic that is alleged to make one person superior to others. They further believe that governments exist to serve the people, not vice versa, and that laws should apply to those who govern as well as to the governed. Modern liberalism in America traces its history to President Franklin Delano Roosevelt, who initiated the New Deal in response to the Great Depression and won an unprecedented four elections. The New Deal coalition established by FDR left a decisive legacy and influenced many future American presidents, including John F. Kennedy. Today, liberalism influences a wide range of social and economic agendas of government. Namely, liberals support such things as reproductive rights for women (including abortion), affirmative action for minority groups historically discriminated against, support for international institutions, support for individual rights over corporate interests, support for universal health care for all citizens, and opposition to tax cuts for the rich.

LIBERALISM DEMANDS PROSPERITY OF CITIZENS

Under the classical definition, liberals advocate a free-market economy without government intervention, and they tend to see the government as a necessary evil. However, a growing distrust of property rights and resulting disproportionate power in the hands of a rich minority at the expense of the working-class majority (today, this working class includes the American middle class) has shaped modern liberal philosophy, modifying its earlier version. Liberal philosophy proclaims that it is not enough that an individual is treated equally under governing law—all must have the same opportunities in life. This puts government in a much more active role, that of providing the same opportunities to all people in order to sustain good democracy. This combination of liberalism and democracy forms contemporary liberal democracy. Most of the world's richest and most powerful nations are liberal democracies with extensive social-welfare programs. Such modern welfare states include countries such as Sweden, Norway, Denmark, Finland, Germany, and Canada. Liberals espouse a wide array of views, depending on their understanding of these principles, but generally support ideas such as constitutionalism, liberal democracy, free and fair elections, human rights, capitalism, and the free exercise of religion. Tracing back to history, classical seventeenth-century liberalism, as a response to autocratic monarchies, promoted the freedom of individual citizens. Eventually, the concepts of "equality" and the "rule of law" were added to the classical liberal doctrine in America as expressed in the Declaration of Independence and the Bill of Rights. The liberalism also advocated a universal humanistic morality. It is the goal of such morality to substitute peaceful behavior for violence, good faith for fraud, considerateness for malice, and cooperation for the dog-eat-dog attitude. These precepts, also in the tenets of world religions, are best expressed in the Christian golden rule: "Do unto others as you would have others do unto you."

INFLUENCE OF JOHN LOCKE'S LIBERALISM ON THE US CONSTITUTION

As American liberalism followed English political ideas, John Locke was especially influential. He, widely known as the father of classical liberalism, was an English philosopher and physician regarded as one of the most influential of Enlightenment thinkers. Locke believed that human nature is characterized by reason and tolerance. The political philosophy of Locke begins with the central notion that persons in "a state of nature" would willingly come together to form a state. Locke believed that people would still live in fear of one another in this state of nature in spite of their ability to reason. It is because of this fear of others that individuals would come together and form a state so that society would provide a neutral judge to protect the lives, liberty, and property of those who live within the civil society. Locke employed the concept of natural rights and social contract based on rule of law. And the rules were subject to the consent of the governed. He emphasized that under the rule of law private individuals must preserve a fundamental right to life, liberty, and property because in a natural state, all people are equal and independent, and everyone has a natural right to defend his "life, health, liberty, or possessions." This became the basis for the phrase in the American Declaration of Independence: "life, liberty, and the pursuit of happiness." Undoubtedly Locke created what would become the philosophical source for the founding principles of the United States. The Enlightenment period was an intellectually thriving time in America during the eighteenth century (1715–89), especially as it related to the American Revolution on the one hand and the European Enlightenment on the other. Influenced by the scientific revolution of the seventeenth century and the humanist period during the Renaissance, the Enlightenment took scientific reasoning and applied it to human nature, society, and even religion.

LIBERALISM AND PURSUIT OF HAPPINESS FOR ALL

Gradually, liberal governments became established in many nations across Europe, Latin America, and North America. Liberal ideas spread even further in the twentieth century, when liberal democracies triumphed in two world wars and survived major ideological challenges from fascism and communism. Today, liberalism in its many forms remains as a powerful political force and influences people's thinking on major continents. Many liberals turned into socialists or conservatives toward the end of the nineteenth century and in the early twentieth century. Others became social liberals, valuing capitalism with a strong government to protect the poor. Also stemming from liberalism is the birth of social democracy—a brand of liberalism awakening to the fact that the market economy alone cannot supply fundamental human necessities to all citizens of society, who require a minimum income to purchase food, clothes, housing, and access to health services. Undoubtedly human reasoning brought a unanimous consensus that strong governments are needed to guarantee those needs. Today, we see this new liberalism (named social democracy) stand as a continuum of philosophical evolution since Aristotle, who asserted that the end of civic virtue is the happiness of citizens.

CIVIC VIRTUE OF REPUBLICANISM

Alongside earlier liberalism, early republicanism was a political ideology in opposition to monarchy and tyranny. To put it differently, republicanism is the ideology of governing a nation as a republic, where the head of state is appointed by means of elections. Republicans hold that a political system must be founded upon the rule of law, the rights of individuals, and the sovereignty of the people. The political ideology is also closely connected to the idea of civic virtue—the responsibility of citizens to their republic. With little doubt, there were a number of theorists behind this, such as Aristotle, Polybius, and Cicero, and their ideas became the essential core of classical Republicanism. The ideology of republicanism blossomed during the Italian Renaissance, most notably in Florence. Classical republicanism is built around concepts of civil society and civic virtue. Devoid of these crucial principles, republicanism is no more than a policing state with the emphasis on law and order. Sadly, the modern Republicanism in America dropped the noble ideas of republicanism stressed by Aristotle and other classical republican theorists—happiness of all citizens—but hastily picked up the idea of Edmund Burke on government.

EDMUND BURKE'S INFLUENCE ON AMERICAN REPUBLICANISM

Edmund Burke (1729–97) wan an Irish political thinker and parliamentarian whose ideas became a major component of Republican values in America today. The Republican Party's beliefs strikingly resemble Burke's ideas of government and religion—no wonder he is often regarded as the father of modern conservatism in America. Burke argued that if man or woman, naïvely fascinated with his or her own limited creativity and intrigued by his or her own radical designs, continues down that radical path of private atheism and public secularism, he would lose all sense of those things greater than himself. Religion, for Burke, is a national cement that holds assurance of trust and each individual citizen's responsibility to a higher moral authority. There can be no pursuit of virtue without recognition of the transcendent power that embodies it, just as there can be no fulfillment in life without tribute to

Him who bestowed it. Religion, in Burke's view, fosters a national character and a culture of morality, both which benefit even those who do not strictly adhere to either. Such a principle encourages deference to transcendent universal truths that constitute the wisdom of God and thus constitute universal law. Burke's conservatism highlights the virtues of prudence, moderation, and humility, and the importance of religion and tradition. He argued that history exists as a continuum, and man as a political creature, finds affinity not only with those around him presently but also with those in the past whose shoulders he stands upon and those of posterity whose foundations he will buttress. Insofar as religion and tradition are concerned, Burke's arguments are very formidable and invite no disagreement. His shortfall, however, lies in the equality issue. For Burke, equality before the law and equality before God are indisputable, but equality of material condition is a chimerical dream. Simply put, the conservatives seek liberty, not equality. As a Christian, Burke acknowledged a certain moral equality of humankind "that is to be found by virtue in all conditions." But egalitarianism as a political program, he opposed on two grounds. First, according to Burke, it is unjust because it encourages envy and inevitably levels people down, since leveling them up is impossible. Second, equality undermines the natural order of things, nature being hierarchical. Burke believed that political equality is against nature; social equality is against nature, and economic equality is against nature. Hence, according to him, the idea of equality is subversive of political, social, and economic order. He claimed that the ambitious elites use equality as a pretext to reallocate resources to themselves. At best, well-intentioned people see equality as no more than a benign aspiration. They think it would be just in theory but, of course, not when applied to them personally in practice, lest this endanger their own privileges. Such were the venomous arguments of Burke that solidified the beliefs of many conservatives who are quite wealthier than the American majority commoners.

Burke entirely misled his audience with the rejection of equality. Equality is not a material concept of quantity or volume on a metric scale; equality represents an equitable claim based on the divine proportion that is necessary to maintain the harmony and peace of any society on Earth.

A metaphor may help support my argument against Burke's view. When a big pine tree with sagging branches is blocking the sunlight, it deprives the small flowers in the garden from happy blooming. Does a rosebush want to be a pine tree? No. It only claims the sunlight that is equally and equitably distributed in the garden so that it can bloom as a rosebush. A good gardener would trim the tree that's been sagging by its own weight and blocking the sun. We must be mindful of divine proportion or golden ratio (Φ) in social, economic, and political, as well as personal conducts, because this law safeguards human happiness and civilization. And of course, beauty and harmony are the other side of equation. Thus, in political reasoning, divine proportion can mean a virtuous government using human intellect to add, subtract, multiply, and divide, morally on a microscale, to see what makes the most sensible happiness for all—for this is the duty of none other than the government.

Burke's notion of civic virtue is lopsided toward the governed—that is, citizens. His assertion on making a nation "one family, one body, one heart and soul" not only implies authoritarian government but also suggests the moral obligation of citizens to serve the nation before happiness of their own, which is aggressively adopted by the US Republican Party via its emphasis on patriotism. Such a notion of national interest is the antithesis of Aristotelian republicanism, which stands upon the principle of stewardship of government, or it being responsible for its citizens' happiness. Is it a true civic virtue of citizens to sacrifice their own happiness to support the national interest? Virtuous politicians should ask themselves what the true national interest should be. The national interest of the republic, by necessity, must reflect the wishes of its people. If the government is unfamiliar with the people it governs and their wishes, it cannot effectively serve those people in any kind of a meaningful way. However, Burke distinguishes between national interest and the wishes of the people as two separate entities. And thus, on this level, Burke's theories on representative government are rather misplaced. Such a system often, not only increases distrust of its people, but also leads the nation to an unstable and unprogressive society. Burke seemed to forget that in order for a human body to stay healthy, the life of every cell in the body has to be well managed—that is, only the well-balanced happiness of its citizens can sustain the peaceful balance of the nation. Thus, inarguably the primary national interest is to serve its citizens for their happiness.

CHRISTIAN INFLUENCE ON REPUBLICANISM

There has been a general division between liberalism and conservatism over what the best civic virtues should be. No matter what one's political ideologies may be, the fundamental human traits identified in a good outcome are always the noble characteristics of individuals. Therefore, it has been cautioned throughout history that ideological ideas alone are not a sufficient guidance for human happiness and civilization—or to judge absolute right or wrong unless human virtues are well formed. In the early days of American history, Christians with great zeal and enthusiasm wanted to bring God into government. They thought they'd brought their spiritual dreams down from the heavens. For example, here is an excerpt from John O'Sullivan on "manifest destiny" from 1839:

"The far-reaching, the boundless future will be the era of American greatness. In its magnificent domain of space and time, the nation of many nations is destined to manifest to mankind the excellence of divine principles; to establish on earth the noblest temple ever dedicated to the worship of the most high—the sacred and the true. Its floor shall be a hemisphere—its roof the firmament of the star-studded heavens, and its congregation, an union of many republics, comprising hundreds of happy millions, calling, owning no man master, but governed by God's moral law of equality, the law of brotherhood—of peace and good will amongst men.

"Yes, we are the nation of progress, of individual freedom, of universal enfranchisement. Equality of rights is the cynosure of our union of States, the grand exemplar of the correlative equality of individuals...We must onward to the fulfillment of our mission...to the entire development of the principle of our organization...freedom of conscience, freedom of person, freedom of trade and business pursuits, universality of freedom and equality. This is our high destiny, and in nature's eternal, inevitable decree of cause and effect we must accomplish it. All this will be our future history, to establish on earth the moral dignity and salvation of man...Who, then, can doubt that our country is destined to be the great nation of futurity?"[38]

The conception of "manifest destiny" was, in fact, a broader expression of the belief that America's mission was to spread goodwill and peace to the world. Under republican democracy during O'Sullivan's time, equal prosperity was of the utmost importance for citizens as well as government, although the republican ideas of freedom of trade and business pursuits began to influence national politics at the same time by supporting more of the wealthy and moneyed interests.

HOW AMERICAN CIVIC VIRTUE POLARIZED INTO TWO MAJOR POLITICAL PARTIES

Eventually in the United States, Democratic-Republicans had to split, and a separate Republican Party emerged in the 1850s. The Republican Party, in the past two centuries, has gradually broadened the term "manifest destiny" toward expansionism, patriotism, and capitalism combined with military power—even though a strong desire for domination and expansion of power is not an American necessity nor an intention of its people. The majority of American people cherish democratic freedom and strongly believe in happiness and peace for all citizens of the nation and world. They oppose the heavy budget of aggressive military expenditure when defense industry and large corporations push the government into military interventions overseas for their own self-interest, hoping the intervention will help their business

---

38 John O'Sullivan, "The Great Nation of Futurity," *The United States Democratic Review* 6, no. 23 (1839): 426–30.

expansion. Recent wars and military interventions have served the interests of corporations and imperialists but damaged the true national interest and well-being of the nation's own people. The resulting effects include the mounting national-budget deficit and increasing poverty in the nation. Poverty means the unaffordability of the fundamentals needed for human living in mod-ernized society, such as food, shelter, medical care, and education. The hu-manistic morality of Christ, which reflects the divine-proportion law of the universe, clearly commands us to rectify this problem. Those who have caused poverty have the responsibility to mend it; thus, if the government enacted ineffective policies to cause the impoverishment of its citizens, it is the govern-ment's obligation to change its ways and solve the problem it has caused. The Republican thinkers perhaps did not foresee how the freedom of trade and business pursuits, allowing the amassing of wealth by a small number of peo-ple, would deprive others and eventually cripple the nation. The Republicans blindly believe that social progress is primarily credited to individuals of mega wealth as evidenced by GDP growth.[39] They are shortsighted by the fact that highly concentrated wealth in a few rich hands is inimical to the well-being and prosperity of the nation, turning the clock back to feudal society where the government protects the rich and the majority of common people live serf-like, with few rights and little property.

In contrast, the Democratic Party always has favored liberal positions sup-porting farmers, laborers, labor unions, and religious and ethnic minorities. It has opposed unregulated business and finance, and favored progressive-income taxes. In other words, the liberal philosophy is the backbone of the Democratic Party, standing for liberal democracy. Liberals and the Democratic Party emphasize individual freedom from want, which underscores the right to an adequate standard of living for everyone. They are broadly talking about

---

39 **Gross domestic product (GDP):** GDP is commonly used as an indicator of the economic health of a country, as well to gauge a country's standard of living. GDP is not intended to gauge material well-being of every citizen of the nation but mostly serves as a measure of a nation's pro-ductivity. It reflects the monetary value of all the finished goods and services produced domesti-cally in a specific time period, calculated as GDP = C + G + I + NX, where C is equal to all private consumption or consumer spending in a nation's economy, G is the sum of government spending, I is the sum of all the country's businesses spending on capital; and NX is the nation's total net exports, calculated as total exports minus total imports.

economic freedom and equality for all. We, as a nation, can direct our moral compass toward a path consistent with humanistic aims, with or without a religious principle, so that our relational behaviors can ethically maximize happiness and minimize sufferings. To do what is the best for the people and nation, the humanistic morality is the backbone of all human relationships and affairs, making it the most important principle not only for the individuals of society but also for those governments entrusted with stewardship to achieve the goal of happiness.

DIVERGENT PATHS OF REPUBLICAN AND DEMOCRATIC PHILOSOPHIES (CONSERVATIVE VERSUS LIBERAL)

The universal principle convinces us that all humans are essentially equal in the grace of God. In the light of this principle, let's briefly review the current ideologies of the Republican and Democratic parties, reflecting on God's harmonic law.

> **Republican beliefs:** "We're fortunate to live in America; the Republican Party believes that the United States has been blessed with a unique set of individual rights and freedoms available to all. You can be what you are and become what you are capable of becoming. The Republican Party is inspired by the power and ingenuity of the individual to succeed through hard work, family support, and self-discipline."[40]

> **Democratic beliefs:** "For over two hundred years, Democrats have stood for the idea that wealth and status should not be an entitlement to rule. Democrats recognize that our country and our economy are strongest when they provide opportunity for all Americans—when we grow our country from the bottom up. We remember that our country was sculpted by immigrants and slaves, and their children and grandchildren. Even today, it is our diversity above all else that

---

40 Source: www.gop.com.

provides us with our enduring strength. Democrats believe that each of us has an obligation to each other, to our neighbors and our communities. Each of us has a role to play in creating our future—and while we have made great progress as a nation, we know that our work is never done."[41]

The underlying philosophy of democracy in America is liberalism. Liberalism is the belief in the importance of liberty and equal rights. Liberalism is the commitment to the freedom of the individual and the preservation of human dignity in any given or changing social situation. Liberalism certainly does not mean freedom and dignity only for a privileged class but personal freedom and human dignity for all. Liberalism is not anarchism but an idea of peaceful coexistence in an equal society as described in divine proportion (Φ). In this respect, the Democratic Party is more aligned with humanistic morality as commanded by God's harmonic law.

Modern liberals typically support the Democratic Party principles emphasizing the welfare state and a mixed economy.[42] In a welfare state, the government has the responsibility for the well-being of its citizens by ensuring that a minimum standard of living is within everyone's reach—turning humanistic morality into civil rights, which makes social welfare a legitimate political and moral claim. Welfare does not refer to charity, sympathy, or pity of the rich. The idea of civil rights makes social welfare a sovereign goal for social equality and justice in the society. The welfare morality is not just a philosophical idea but a humanistic requisite to be practiced by all. Such practice can be translated into the provision of universal and free education; universal medical care; insurance against disability, sickness, and unemployment; family allowances for income supplement; and old-age pensions at an acceptable level. Liberals emphasize equality and, therefore, support institutions that defend against extreme economic inequality. They believe that true freedom and

---

41 Source: www.democrats.org/about/our_party.

42 **Mixed economy:** A mixed economy represents an economic system that includes a mixture of capitalism and socialism. This type of economic system combines private economic freedom and centralized economic planning and government regulation.

peace exist when necessities like education, health care, and opportunity are available to all. John F. Kennedy defined a liberal as follows:

> Someone who looks ahead and not behind, someone who welcomes new ideas without rigid reactions, someone who cares about the welfare of the people, their health, their housing, their schools, their jobs, their civil rights, and their civil liberties, someone who believes we can break through the stalemate and suspicions that grip us in our policies abroad, if that is what they mean by a "liberal," then I'm proud to say I'm a liberal.[43]

It is, however, obvious that not all American people appreciate the core of liberal ideals, and many hurried off to the conservative camp without understanding the deep, hidden meaning of what conservatism stands for. Conservatives assert national strength and pride, believing and insisting that this nation's people and form of government (republic) are truly suitable. The "people" they are referring to are those who do well in economic survival but not the poor or helpless (although they marginally include the poor in a symbolical gesture). Conservatives, as defenders of civic order, are hostile to both tyranny and lawlessness, domestic or international. Their hostility has been well demonstrated by the meddling in foreign affairs with military interventions (in the Middle East, for example). Conservatives believe that free enterprise and individual initiative have brought this nation unparalleled opportunity and prosperity. They believe that the nation's continued success and long-term survival depend on productive citizens and their enterprises, not the government. Under Republican policy, national strength or success is primarily dependent on large private businesses' profit and income in order to increase the national balance sheet (translated into GDP growth). In turn, they think the GDP per capita indicates the prosperity of the country and the country's standard of living. However, we must understand that the GDP per capita income is a misleading barometer in measuring national prosperity or standard of living, for it does not take into account the real cost of living. This probusiness attitude of

---

43 Source: Acceptance of the New York Liberal Party nomination (September 14, 1960).

Conservatives (Republicans) is nothing new: it's been present all along from the very inception of the formation of America by the founding fathers. The relatively simple American landscape of the colonial age has changed rapidly since then, with a population growth from less than four million to over three hundred million with multicultural and multireligious beliefs. Another spectacular change since then is human longevity. People used to live only forty to fifty years in the earlier colonial time; now that longevity is stretched to a hundred years. In this pluralistic society with large population growth, a staggering number of citizens are unable to participate in production as long as wealth is concentrated in the few hands of the wealthy, who control the production and labor for their own profit—that is, until the government counteracts to reallocate the wealth for the creation of opportunities for those helpless and unproductive citizens. In the end, a nation with equitable distribution of wealth would be able to reap true prosperity for all its citizens. In other words, the true prosperity of the nation represents the sum of individual prosperity of all people of the nation, not just of the rich class. National power primarily depending on a small number of wealthy citizens at the expense of its poor majority eventually collapses without question. How it will collapse is beyond the scope of discussion in this book. However, the definite possibility of such a calamity is looming.

GOVERNMENT'S STEWARDSHIP

When we talk about the responsibility of government, we are referring to none other than the responsibility of Congress—the driving force of the nation of America. The Congress is the heart and soul of America and thus carries the responsibility of stewardship for national welfare. Regardless of party-line ideological differences, the American public demands a united Congress in shaping policies for the people, not for the class. Although each congressman and congresswoman was elected by his or her own small subgroup with specific interests, he or she must assume national responsibility once sworn into office. In reality, however, most of members of Congress, preoccupied with arm wrestling for hegemony among themselves, seem to be completely oblivious to the mounting poverty of large number of citizens. It's not surprising to see Americans' confidence in Congress at only 6 percent, shown on Gallup Poll as of June 2016. The main dissatisfaction with congressional behavior lies in its economic decisions on the welfare of its people. Congress has authority over revenue and spending policies; therefore, people expect congressional actions to create more revenue via higher taxation to the rich and to allocate the revenue where it's mostly needed: that is, reductions of deficit and poverty. These simple actions, however, seem unacceptable to the congressional majority. Republican members of Congress oppose a tax increase for the rich. At the same time, despite the fact that citizens are gravely concerned about the fiscal responsibility of government in balancing the budget by reducing the deficit amount, Congress is not willing to cut the military budget to the minimum. Instead, Republicans are proposing, as a solution to balancing the national budget, spending cuts of domestic-welfare programs, education, and all other domestic programs that help citizen well-being.

Many Christian Republicans tend to think that winning economic wealth is God's blessing and that falling into poverty is God's curse. Therefore, to them people suffering from poverty who are unproductive are neither valuable to society nor do they deserve compassion from them. So when these poor people commit crimes, under the "civic order" definition, they do not deserve mercy but prison. In the meantime, under the Republican affirmation, military expansion is unquestionably important to strengthen the dominion of the nation in the world; and protecting the rich and their enterprises is of paramount importance in order to guarantee the nation's power and prosperity. Thus, the government must not regulate their capitalistic behavior nor increase their tax but instead give them full freedom of pursuits. One must ask then: Should government leave the super rich alone, watching them erode the economic health of the nation by squeezing the poor while the nation is largely built on Christian principle? We cannot stress too much political moral duty of helping those who can't help themselves and protecting those who can't defend themselves. Such moral commitment is not just based on liberal philosophy but on Congressional mission based on God's law, delivered through

Christ's second commandment (humanistic morality) and divine proportion (Φ) for harmony. One must be reminded that Christianity and political leadership are closely intertwined across the culture and history of America. Of US citizens, 73 percent consider themselves Christians, whether they are liberal or conservatives. And almost 92 percent of the 114 Congress members sworn in in January 2015 are Christian, according to Pew Research Center report. It is worth noting, in such a Christian-dominated country, how American citizens are polarized between liberal and conservative views, which are reflected in the congressional battlefield. I have selected major polemic issues that are part of determinant factors for congressional elections, discussed below.

AFFIRMATIVE ACTION

Liberals point out that because of unequal opportunity, minorities still lag behind whites in all statistical measurements of success. Due to prevalent racism in the past, minorities were deprived of the same education and employment opportunities as whites, and the government must take action to correct this. The affirmative action stretches beyond racial discrimination; in a nutshell, it supports the idea of helping the helpless. It is obviously Christian morality to help one another as brothers and sisters when others are having difficulty. Liberals understand that not everyone can become an entrepreneur or is employable as a healthy laborer in mainstream society; nonetheless, they are still part of our national family and deserve our compassion and care.

When it comes to how conservatives think about race in America, no issue provides a clearer picture of their perspective than affirmative action—that is, conservatives see the issue very differently than liberals. While liberals believe affirmative-action programs create opportunities for blacks and other minorities where they didn't previously exist, conservatives believe they actually serve to foster racism by denying opportunities to whites who are equally qualified. The conservatives also argue that most affirmative-action programs address specific minorities while alienating others, which creates tension and undermines the ideal of racial equality.

THE NATIONAL ECONOMY

Liberals' idea for the national economy is that the government must protect citizens from the greed of big business and its rich beneficiaries. Unlike the private sector, the government must direct its policies toward public interest and regulate all areas of the economy to level the playing field.

Conservatives claim that free-market system, competitive capitalism, and private enterprise create the greatest opportunity and the highest standard of living for all. They believe that free markets produce more economic growth and more jobs than those systems burdened by excessive government regulation. Conservatives don't seem to realize that economic growth is effected only as a part of long-term economic prosperity of human civilization. "Economic prosperity" refers to the concerted actions of government and communities that promote the standard of living and economic health of the nation, whereas "economic growth" is just a phenomenon of market productivity and rise in GDP. Economic growth can be stopped by a long slump when the distribution of wealth is severely blocked for the common people. In other words, the economic growth that largely depends on consumerism will suffer when consumers are too poor to buy goods. Equitable distribution of wealth is therefore a prerequisite for healthy economic growth and for sustainable long-term prosperity for the nation.

Many economists and experts, including the CBO (Congressional Budget Office) and US Census Bureau, have been supplying the public with various statistical records and phenomenal evidences that the unchecked free-market activities of private enterprises have created a huge chasm between the poor and rich in the United States during the past thirty years. The avaricious, unregulated activities on Wall Street ended up bringing the national economy into a deep recession started in 2008, and large corporations are not concerned about welfare for the poor. They're mainly concerned about their own profits and how they can grow more in wealth. When the economy goes bad, the first thing these corporations do is eliminate the jobs of those who live from paycheck to paycheck, creating large unemployment rates. This is the effect of unregulated, free market capitalism. In an unregulated capitalistic society, the poor are always at the mercy of the unsympathetic rich. The 2014 Social

Security Administration records indicate that 51 percent of American workers earned less than $30,000,[44] while 35 percent made less than the national average wage of $46,482. In the same period, average expenditures per American consumer unit were over $53,000 according to US Bureau of Labor Statistics.[45] By looking at these statistics one can't help but conclude that over 50 percent of American citizens are literally living from hand to mouth. Throwing the poor into the poverty ditch is very easy—just take the jobs away from these wage earners. In the meantime, the share of top 20 percent rich Americans in national wealth grew from 85 to 87.7 percent since 2007. Furthermore, the after-tax income of the top 1 percent earnings grew by 281 percent after adjusting for inflation, while income growth for the bottom fifth of earners was only 16 percent between 1979 and 2007[46] as shown in figure 8 below.

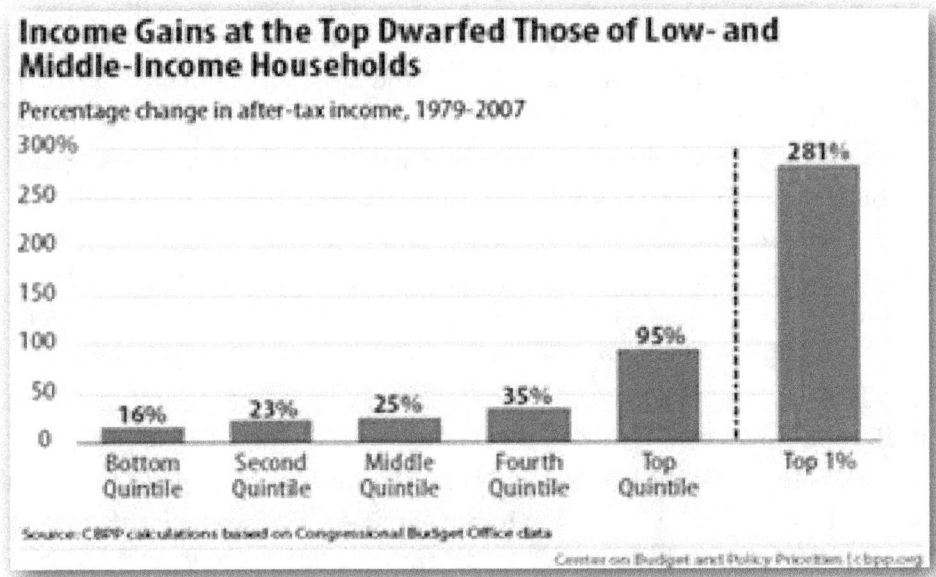

Income Gains at the Top Dwarfed Those of Low- and Middle-Income Households

Percentage change in after-tax income, 1979-2007

Source: CBPP calculations based on Congressional Budget Office data

Center on Budget and Policy Priorities | cbpp.org

Figure 8: Percentage change of income gain since 1979

---

44 Social Security Administration, *Wage Statistics for 2014* (July 24, 2016).

45 Bureau of Labor Statistics, *CONSUMER EXPENDITURES—2014* (September 3, 2015).

46 The Center on Budget and Policy Priorities (CBPP), "Income Gaps between Very Rich and Everyone Else More Than Tripled in Last Three Decades," *New Data Show,* released June 10, 2010.

Now America is divided between the small rich, powerful 1 percent and the large poor, helpless 99 percent by a huge income-growth disparity. How did they get to be so big while the rest of America is struggling? Were those 1 percenters blessed generously and the rest of nation cursed by God?

TAXES

The liberals' position is that wealthy Americans should pay higher taxes, which would enable the government to create jobs and provide welfare programs for those in need—since government programs, in compliance with civil society's rule, provide caring ways to provide for the poor and needy in society. Conservatives argue that lower taxes for everyone and a smaller government with limited power will improve the standard of living for all. They support lower taxes and a smaller government, as they believe lower taxes create more incentive for people to work, save, invest, and engage in entrepreneurial endeavors. They argue that the money is best spent by those who earn it, not the government. The conservatives also argue that government welfare programs encourage people to become dependent and lazy, rather than encouraging work and independence.

In the fourth quarter of 2015, the US government gross debt amounted almost 125 percent of GDP,[47] according to the OECD and "debt held by the public" was 96 percent of GDP. The statistical trend indicates that current debt level is more than twice what it was at the end of 2007 and higher than in any year since 1950. We know that entrepreneurs, investors, and consumers on Main Street fear the consequences of the rising federal debt. The dynamics of a rising federal debt relative to the national economy are portentous to the nation's future. When the gross government debt relative to the size of the economy exceeds a certain threshold, economic growth and job creation will slow down dramatically, according to a National Bureau of Economic

---

47 Source: OECD Statistics—National Accounts, retrieved May 6, 2016.
     There are two components of gross national debt: "Debt held by the public," such as Treasury securities held by investors outside the federal government and "Debt held by government accounts" or intragovernmental debt, such as the Social Security Trust Fund.

Research study by Carmen Reinhart and Kenneth Rogoff.[48] The study ana-lyzed newly compiled data on government debt in forty-four countries span-ning about two hundred years. It found that when debt exceeds the threshold of 90 percent of GDP, the median rate of economic growth falls by about 1 percentage point per year, and the average (mean) rate falls by almost 4 per-centage points.

In the midst of such debt crisis, the four hundred highest-income earn-ers in America paid virtually the same percentage in taxes as people mak-ing $50,000–$75,000 under the Bush tax-cut extension. Those earning more than $10 million a year now pay less in taxes than those making $100,000–$200,000. This clearly indicates that the rich are getting the biggest share of the tax cuts, resulting in a small drop in the federal-taxes-revenue bucket. According to Mr. Warren Buffett, the mega rich people in America pay in-come taxes at a rate of 15 percent on most of their earnings but pay practically nothing in payroll taxes. It's a different story for the middle class: typically, they fall into the 15 and 25 percent income-tax brackets and then are hit with heavy payroll taxes to boot if they are small-business owners. On August 14, 2011, Warren Buffett wrote in a *New York Times* piece that the United States (Congress) should stop "coddling" the rich and raise the top income-tax rate in an effort to reduce the deficit (and already accumulated debt). Similarly, Maurice Lévy, chairman and chief executive of the French adver-tising firm Publicis, said it is only fair that the most privileged members of our society should take up a bigger share of the national burden. Sixteen of France's wealthiest people, including Christophe de Margerie, CEO of the French oil giant Total, signed a petition published in the magazine *Le Nouvel Observateur* urging the French government to tax them more. A group of about fifty wealthy individuals in Germany, who have been campaigning for a higher top tax rate since 2009, welcomed the French petition.

A simple accounting principle tells us that, whether through individual finance management or national fiscal policy, revenue has to be increased to meet demanding expenses to avoid catastrophic consequences. The negative

---

48 Carmen Reinhart and Kenneth Rogoff, *Growth in a Time of Debt* (National Bureau of Economic Research, January 2010).

income or deficit increases liability, which is national debt in our discussion here. When deficits are financed by borrowing from domestic lenders (public debt), the government will incur a liability to repay both the principal and interest amount as per contract, leaving less money available for investing here at home into the building blocks of the nation's economic prosperity. If they are financed by foreigners (external debt), the nation will owe a mushrooming debt to the rest of the world, with growing interest costs that must be met every year. According to the report issued by the Center on Budget and Policy Priorities (CBPP), the 2014 actual spending on interest payments was 7 percent of total federal outlays.

Given the level and composition of taxation and government spending in various sectors, modern economists have been more concerned with the distribution of income across individuals and households. Important theoretical and policy concerns include the relationship between income inequality and economic growth. The 2013 Nobel Prize winner in economics, Robert J. Shiller, stated that rising inequality in the United States and elsewhere is the most crucial problem.[49] No doubt, increasing inequality harms economic growth. The economic inequality of society separating its citizens into economic "elites" and "mass poor" eventually can destroy the nation and its civilization. America today is more unequal than during the Great Depression. Huge numbers of people are economically struggling or insecure, and yet the richest are not willing to share the burden.

To illuminate this point further, I want to highlight actual figures here. The total privately held wealth of the United States in 2009 was approximately $54 trillion, out of which the top 1 percent of the rich owned 34.6 percent, or $19 trillion. During the same time, the US gross debt was almost $12 trillion against $14 trillion of GDP. In other words, the wealth ownership by the top 1 percent rich far exceeds the amount of national debt or GDP. According to an analysis of Federal Reserve data by the Economic Policy Institute, the top 1 percent of Americans by net worth still hold about a third of American wealth today. The super rich folks of America at this juncture need to ponder

---

49 Robert J. Shiller, "Better Insurance against Inequality," *The New York Times, Economic View*, April 12, 2014.

seriously the speech of John F. Kennedy: "Ask not what your country can do for you—ask what you can do for your country."

When the nation is facing an imminent danger of economic collapse, the government is the only steward with full authority to save the nation. In the modern economic environment, governmental functions are expected to expand to cope with the fast evolution of technologies and population growth, embracing equitable distribution of wealth and fair taxation among citizens. The conservatives are attempting to fight for a limited role of government. They frequently quote Thomas Jefferson, who argued that good government is limited government and that limited government encourages our civic happiness. But they seem to pretend to ignore the fact that the limited-government philosophy only has encouraged unfettered greed, leaving the majority of Americans in poor financial health.

As we are fully aware, the government has a vast range of responsibilities for many types of economic issues in contemporary societies. But the ultimate goal of all economic decisions must aim at the happiness of its citizens by helping them achieve the fundamental elements of a good life. In a true sense, the mission of the government is to maintain the divine proportion (golden ratio) of society, for it is the law of balance in the universe, all life forms, and nature. Congress has a critical mission as the driver of our economic locomotive, regardless of differences between Republican and Democratic ideologies, to carry the nation to a safe destination—just as John Adams laid down the moral principle of government, saying: "The happiness of society is the end of government as happiness of the individual is the end of man."[50]

---

50 "Thoughts on Government" was an essay written by John Adams, during the spring of 1776 in response to a resolution of the North Carolina Provincial Congress which requested Adams' suggestions on the establishment of a new government and the drafting of a constitution. Adams says that "Politics is the Science of human Happiness -and the Felicity of Societies depends on the Constitutions of Government under which they live." Many of the ideas put forth in Adams' essay were adopted in December 1776 by the framers of North Carolina's first constitution. For Adams, the purpose of government is to be found in the goal of happiness. Such happiness lies not merely in "ease, comfort, and security" but in virtue, the manly exercise of moral and intellectual excellence. Online text is available at http://www.heritage.org/initiatives/first-principles/primary-sources/john-adams-thoughts-on-government

Such is the bedrock of the congressional mission. America has a government with the ability, authority, and public support needed to counter the forces that are pulling the nation apart, although at any given time a small segment of citizens may denounce anything the federal government does as a threat to individual liberty or basic rights. The modern Tea Party movement has deep roots in this history. In fact, antistatism (opposition to government intervention) and a mistrust of government power go all the way back to the neurotic anti-Federalists who feared a monarchy and opposed the Constitution because they saw it concentrating too much authority in the central government. However, the elected government shouldn't hesitate to act upon its duty to attain the desired end—that is, the happiness of the greatest number of people and the nation's prosperity. Liberals believe in a strong representative government that protects and promotes equal opportunity for all people in the nation. It is the job of the government to help solve social ills and to protect the civil liberties of all. The role of the government should be to protect every citizen and guarantee that no person is in poverty by solving the problem of inequality. Imposing higher taxation on the rich certainly is a very fair and sensible way to balance the budget, as well as help the poor by enabling them to become productive citizens.

WELFARE

Conservatives (Republicans) oppose long-term welfare, contending that it allows poor people to remain dependent on the government and engenders indolence. Further, they assert that they shouldn't have sympathy for the poor since poor people's misery is the manifestation of God's curse. It's quite shocking to hear such unsympathetic remarks from Christian conservatives. It seems to me that the real curse might befall them for violating Christ's second greatest commandment: "Love your neighbor as yourself." While the Christian conservatives believe the benevolent-community myth, they are willing to ignore the most important Christian principle: sharing the blessings of wealth with brothers and sisters who are in need. Liberals, in contrast, visualize the American community as inclusive of everyone in it and believe in: "I am my brother's keeper and my sister's keeper." Liberals speak of the common good and have a set of values that reflect their belief: "We're in this together." Conservatives use a different moral standard: "What's in it for me?"

SOCIAL SECURITY

Liberals insist that the social-security system should be protected at all costs. They insist that a reduction in future benefits is not an acceptable option and that social security provides a safety net for the nation's poor and needy. Conservatives contend that the social security system is in serious financial trouble and that we urgently need to make major changes to the current system via a privatized system. The idea behind "privatization" is that workers are responsible for their future benefits; by putting their retirement funds into government-supervised private accounts, workers manage their own savings. This is the essence of the social security reform the Republican Party is proposing. This assumption can be addressed for those who are actively employed with decent earnings and capable of investing their own money for future retirement. In reviewing their argument, it is worthwhile to mention the average earnings of workers in America. According to the US Bureau of Labor Statistics, the average weekly salary of the American worker as of the first quarter of 2016 was $830. The 2014 Social Security Administration records indicate that 51 percent of American workers earned less than $30,000, while 50 percent made less than the national average wage of $64,481. In the same period, average expenditures per American consumer unit were over $53,000 according to the US Bureau of Labor Statistics. Is there enough extra money for low-waged people to save money for their retirement?

In 1937, the Social Security Act was drafted during Franklin Roosevelt's first term as part of the New Deal. It was originally intended to protect American citizens from a perilous life of financial strife, including old age, poverty, unemployment, and the burdens of widows and fatherless children. The original intent of this act was to take care of those who couldn't take care of themselves. According to a monthly statistical snapshot released by the Social Security Administration in March 2016, the average monthly Social Security retirement benefit for January 2016 was $1,341. This meager amount is what poor Americans are dependent on if they have no other supplemental supports, such as a pension and other company-paid extras. Saving for retirement is hard. The latest Retirement Confidence Survey in 2016 by the Employee Benefit Research Institute (EBRI) reported that 26 percent of Americans have less than $1,000 in retirement savings, excluding their home. Further, a whopping 64 percent have less than $50,000. Most of these workers say they simply cannot afford to save for the future.

With too much focus on long-term national macroeconomic projections, very little concern about income adequacy for citizens has been brought up by either party of the US Congress. In 2015, the US government spent 6.7 percent of GDP on the pension, which is below the OECD average of 7.9 percent. It should be noted that in most of OECD nations, the government assumes the responsibility offering generous benefits for average wage earners in their old age. Not surprisingly, the United States is the sixth from the bottom among the thirty-five OECD nations.[51] For the financial security of older people, according to the OECD report comparing to other countries, the United States was ranked sixth lowest having 22 percent of pensioners living below the poverty line against the OECD average of 12.6 percent.[52] In most of OECD countries, taking care of people who are old and unable to work is considered part of the very definition of a civilized society. In the four largest Nordic countries (Denmark, Norway, Sweden, and Finland) that are members of OECD, for instance, there is a housing allowance in addition to the old-age benefit, which is of great significance to retirees with low income. When housing allowance is added, the retiree's income level can almost rise up to an average worker's income in America.

On a final note on this issue of old-age benefit, let's not forget that the senior generation is part of our national family who contributed to the society equally by their hard labor. They equally participated in production to grow

---

51 OECD nations are retrieved from http://www.oecd.org/about/members and partners.
52 OECD and G20 Indicators, Pensions at a Glance 2013.

the economy, which became the fertilizer of our current civilization. They were the torch carriers toward current civilization, fostering the way for new generations. Thus, it is only proper to respect and honor them, and to take care of them in their old age. In other words, the welfare is nothing but a duty of society and government.

EDUCATION

Liberals think public schools are the best way to educate children. They believe that the government should provide additional funds to existing public schools, raising teacher salaries and reducing class size. Conservatives say that vouchers will give all parents the right to choose good schools for their children, not just those who can afford private schools. Setting aside such frivolous debate, we can note that many advanced countries in Europe offer free or almost-free education up to college level. The children are the future of our national destiny; thus, their education is the nation's responsibility. This human capital must be protected by the government. Education is not a commodity to be purchased and sold in the market, but it's societal responsibility to foster the evolution of human life on Earth. Thus, education is not a privilege but a duty for all humankind.

HEALTH CARE

Liberals believe that every American citizen has a right to affordable health care and that the government should provide equal health care benefits for all, regardless of their ability to pay. There are millions of Americans who can't afford health care and are deprived of this basic right. Conservatives argue that free and low cost government-run programs (socialized medicine) result in higher costs, with everyone receiving the same poor-quality health care. Thus, Conservatives believe health care should remain privatized and that the problem of uninsured individuals should be addressed and solved within the free-market health-care system. In their opinion, the government shouldn't control health care.

Many advanced and developed nations in the world have already recognized that free health care is a fundamental right for every citizen of a given society. Not surprisingly, the United States has the worst medical-benefit system among all advanced nations, according to a report by the Commonwealth Fund, a New York–based private foundation focused on health. Among adults with chronic conditions, almost half (45 percent) of population with below-average incomes in the United States reported that they went without needed care in the past year because of costs, compared with just 4 percent in the Netherlands. The lower-income US adults with chronic conditions were significantly more likely than those in the six other advanced countries surveyed to report not going to the doctor when they're sick, not filling a prescription, or not getting recommended follow-up care because of costs.

WAR ON TERROR/TERRORISM

Conservatives believe that terrorism poses the greatest threat to the nation. According to Republicans, the United Nations has repeatedly failed in its essential mission to promote world peace and human rights. The conservatives therefore insist that history shows that the United States, not the United Nations, is the global force for spreading freedom, prosperity, tolerance, and peace. In their view, the United States should never place troops under UN control, and the US military should always wear the US uniform, not that of UN peacekeepers. Such an arrogant attitude prompted Republicans to take the law in their own hands to invade Iraq. They have been allocating an unforgivable amount of money into the defense budget, pushing down domestic-welfare programs to the last priority on list.

The United States had the highest military expenditures in 2015,[53] again ranking number one in military supremacy in the world. The United States, in fiscal year 2015, allocated 54 percent of all federal discretionary spending, or a total of $598.5 billion for military expenditure.[54] The overburdened,

---

53 Source: Stockholm International Peace Research Institute (April 2016).
54 Source: OMB, National Priorities Project, FY 2015 Mandatory and Discretionary Spending.

disproportionate US military expenditure has pushed the national debt to an intolerable level, leaving the nation on the brink of economic disaster. It is worth mentioning here the military spending of Saudi Arabia. Its annual budget allocated to military expenditure represents 13.7 percent while the US expenditure represented 3.3 percent of the GDP for 2015.[55] These figures offer some insight into what's going on in the world today. The United States aggressively seeks to weaken and divide the Islamic world for itself without resorting to any cooperation from the United Nations. In the meantime, the Islamic world of Middle East tries to stand up against the aggression of American military intervention by fortifying the region with equally powerful military forces. It should be acknowledged that the US-military presence in the Middle East has been quite unpopular nationally and internationally. According to a BBC poll, most respondents said that America provokes more conflict than it prevents in the region. The poll also found that overall views of the United States have worsened around the world while Germany received the highest positive view. [56]

Liberals know that the United Nations promotes peace and human rights, meaning the United States has a moral and a legal obligation to support these principles. America shouldn't act alone as a powerful arrogant nation but as a member of the world community. The liberal approach to international relations emphasizes cooperation among countries to promote economic interdependence and global harmony. Additionally, liberals reject the notion that war is an inevitable product of international relations, while stressing economic, societal, environmental, and technological issues when discussing national interests. Liberals believe that nonstate actors (nongovernmental organizations) are important players in international relations and must be considered along with the state actors (governments). While states may be considered sovereign, in reality other actors such as multinational corporations, terrorist groups, nongovernmental organizations, and other transnational actors are all important and relevant. Liberalism stresses that many factors are at work in international relations and that the many

---

55 SIPRI, "Trends in World Military Expenditure, 2015"
56 BBC Poll, conducted in June 2014.

interactions among state and nonstate actors can be managed only by an international institution such as the United Nations, where members agree on accepted norms and rules for international relations.

RELIGION'S ROLE IN GOVERNMENT

Liberals support the separation of church and state. Conservatives argue that the phrase "separation of church and state" is not in the US Constitution. Conservative Christians (especially fundamentalists and evangelical Christians, who are predominantly Republicans) criticize the moral decline of American society, the loss of positive values and virtues in everything from our schools to our music, the destructive influence of Hollywood and the drug culture, and the decadence of much of our contemporary cultural life. They are concerned that the United States is no longer a Christian nation. They resent the decline of religious influence in public life as a result of judicial decisions that enforce the principle of the separation of church and state—that bar religious emblems from government premises and that limit prayer and religious instruction in public schools. Much of this valid social criticism of conservative Christians is well received by general Christians. But the fundamentalist approach by conservative Republicans to moral values is quite un-Christian, being authoritarian, rigid, and punitive. They assert their authority by citing selected phrases of the Bible, taking passages out of their historical, cultural, and linguistic context. These folks are using those carefully selected passages to assert their ethical and moral positions, which sharply contradict the true Christian moral principle—humanistic morality. They value individual interests over community, national interests (world dominance) over the welfare of the citizens, and corporate and individual wealth over common good in human society.

In a nutshell, the only way a society can measure its true justice and well-being is by mirroring its governmental decisions through the universal law of harmony and God's wisdom. Religious beliefs have been an important part of political discourse from the very beginning of the nationhood of

America. It is unimportant, however, whether government institutions officially accept Christianity as a national religion or not, so long as the people in it practice their religious spirit to do good for others. The citizens do not expect Congress just to protect the super rich's interests, creating crony capitalism, but rather to scrutinize the citizens' desire under the moral-beacon light, providing for the welfare of the people. Most Republican members of Congress are unfortunately defenders of the rich, who praise the free-market economy but who shun discussions on humanistic morality that protects the happiness of all citizens. Contemporary capitalism carries with it inherently selfish interests that ignore human virtue or morality; thus, in a capitalist-dominated society, the divine proportion or golden ratio (ϕ) is completely absent. Consequently, social harmony and peace become perilously jeopardized, with the government turning a deaf ear to the requirements of civic morality for citizens' happiness.

The citizens want to look up to the Congress as a trusted champion of national morality, leading the governed toward what is good, and what is good for the nation, as well as teaching what is evil and what harms the nation. To instruct the citizens regarding the good, to lead them toward it, and to protect them from evildoings are all part of the government's moral duty. The government—more specifically, Congress—is the steward safeguarding national civilization. This civilization is much more profound and broader than simple national security and interests. The civilization is not defined by mere wealth, personal comfort, and pleasure or by science and technology or even by self-expression and self-preservation. Rather, it is defined by spiritual maturity displayed in the virtues of human beings, both public and private. It denotes the equal prosperity of all in harmonious coexistence. Civilization nurtures sublime and elegant beauties in culture, such as music, the arts, and poised human attitudes that inspire a peaceful soul of humankind in exquisite ways. The civilization blooms in a clean environment, where a society values gentleness, brotherhood, and interdependence more than self-interest and self-reliance as social mores. And then civilization is for all of us and many future generations to enjoy.

Good law helps curb human greed, while human virtue helps shaping good law, the law for the nation. Well-framed law with humanistic morality helps us make the best use of our freedom by guiding us to avoid both excess and deficiency. Without the moral backbone of law, we are deprived of our best protector. Those who are frightened by the moral pedagogy of law seem not to understand that the natural rights of citizens can be oppressed by an excessive freedom to villains who impoverish the helpless. Good law provides ample room for freedom and liberty, but a law estranged from humanistic morality and ethical considerations tends to side with evil forces such as greed and selfishness.

Humanistic morality itself is an intangible system that has no authoritative judges and no decision procedure to provide solid guidance to action in all moral situations. Thus, inevitably we have to rely on policy makers who can translate humanistic morality into law. This means congressmen and congresswomen are elected as moral agents and that citizens expect them to be rational persons who can create good law, guiding the national morality with humanism. In this sense, the morality applied to all public laws reflects the sense of morality being defined by moral agents who have the capacity to reason as rational beings. A good public law, defined as national morality, incorporates the essential feature as to what kinds of actions morality prohibits, requires, discourages, encourages, and allows to achieve the national goal—or common good denoted as happiness for all. Humanistic morality, being a universal principle to achieve the common goal of happiness for all, defines right conduct for all citizens under the good law. That way, the law enacted by the government is both an expression and shaper of national conscience and civilization.

The American founding fathers clearly recognized that humanistic morality is God's will and therefore an indispensable part of politics of a Christian nation. In fact, from their perspective, politics was simply morality applied to the public domain, to the public's business. The founders of America promulgated a new Constitution for their fledgling nation to fight against the morally evil and politically unjust actions of King George III. The founders wanted the nation to be moral, obeying God's will—that is, universal harmonic law.

They wanted the nation's laws to be a reflection of God's law, with moral excellence. What they envisioned in the nation was virtuous government. I want to say, regardless of what form of government citizens decide to select, their confidence in that government's policy makers and their noble character is the strongest indicator of governmental civic virtue,[57] which shapes the nation's destiny.

---

57 Civic virtue means that both citizens and their leaders have to live modest lives, working hard and putting the common welfare above their own interests. Lucius Quinctius Cincinnatus (519–430 BC) of the Roman Republic is seen as a model of civic virtue. He often has been cited as an example of outstanding leadership, service to the greater good, lack of personal ambition, and modesty. Cincinnatus was a hard-working farmer with only four acres of land. When the messengers found him, he was quietly plowing his fields. Because he loved his country, he left his plow to go to Rome and lead the army in battle. His army defeated the enemy and saved Rome. Cincinnatus was honored and praised by his people. But when the battle was over, he did not try to remain a dictator of his country. He did not want continued fame. Instead, he returned to his home and his life as a citizen. By returning to his home, Cincinnatus showed that he valued being a citizen of Rome more than he valued fame and personal power. This was a strong example of civic virtue during the earlier period of the Roman Republic.

Chapter 7

DECLINE OF REPUBLICAN CIVIC VIRTUE

JOHN ADAMS'S CHRISTIAN VIRTUE

The second president of the United States, John Adams (1735–1826), signer of the Declaration of Independence, often pondered the issue of civic virtue.[58] He agreed with the Greeks and Romans that public virtue cannot exist without private virtue, and that public virtue is the only foundation of republics. Adams worried that a businessman might have financial interests that conflicted with republican duty; indeed, he was especially suspicious of banks. He decided that history had taught that the spirit of commerce (materialism) is incompatible with purity of heart and greatness of soul, which is necessary for a happy republic.

Before becoming the second president of the United States, John Adams served as the vice president under President George Washington. Prior to that, John Adams was a signer of the Declaration of Independence as a delegate from Massachusetts. The first two US presidents were patrons of religion: George Washington was an Episcopal vestryman and John Adams described himself as "a church-going animal." Both offered strong support for religion.

---

58 John Adams, *A Dissertation on the Canon and Feudal Law.* Source: TeachingAmericanHistory. org.

In his farewell address of September 1796, Washington called religion, as the source of morality, a necessary spring of popular government[59], while Adams claimed that while statesmen may plan and speculate for liberty, it is religion and morality alone that can establish the principles upon which freedom can securely stand.

THOMAS JEFFERSON'S INTELLECTUAL VIRTUE

On the other hand, Thomas Jefferson (1743–1826), the third president, is generally considered less hospitable to religious institutions than his predecessors, with his scientific bent, but he did seek to organize his thoughts on religious principles. He rejected the superstitions and mysticism of Christianity, and even went so far as to edit the gospels, removing the miracles and mysticism of Jesus and leaving only what he deemed to be Jesus's correct moral philosophy. Nonetheless, Jefferson believed in God and used his intellect to recognize how Christian zealotry harmed society more than benefiting it. In his diary, Jefferson noted, "Millions of innocent men, women and children, since the introduction of Christianity, have been burnt, tortured, fined and imprisoned; yet we have not advanced one inch towards uniformity."[60] But evidence of his deep trust in God was seen in Jefferson's own epitaph on his memorial stone that read: "I have sworn upon the altar of God eternal hostility against every form of tyranny over the mind of man."[61]

He had used the term "Democrat-Republican" for his party, and his supporters wanted to use the term Republican as their party name, which would echo the republican values of civic virtue. Revolutionary republicanism was centered on limiting corruption and greed. Virtue was of the utmost

---

59 George Washington, Farewell Address 1796, Yale Law School, Lillian Goldman Law Library.

60 Thomas Jefferson, *Notes on the State of Virginia, Query 17, 157–61*

61 Jeri Ferris, *Thomas Jefferson: Father of Liberty (Trailblazers)* (Carolrhoda Books, 1998).
  Thomas Jefferson to Dr. Benjamin Rush, September 23, 1800, in *The Thomas Jefferson Papers* (Library of Congress, History): "I Have Sworn Upon the Altar of God Eternal Hostility Against Every Form of Tyranny Over the Mind of Man," http://www.history.com/topics/us-presidents/thomas-jefferson.

importance for citizens and representatives. Revolutionaries took a lesson from the Roman Empire (the post-republican period of the ancient Roman civilization); they knew it was necessary to avoid the pitfalls that had destroyed the empire. The republic is sacred; therefore, it is necessary to serve the state in a truly representative way, ignoring self-interest and individual will. Republicanism required the service of those who were willing to give up their own interests for a common good. Virtuous citizens needed to be strong defenders of liberty and challenge the corruption and greed in government. The duty of the virtuous citizen became a foundation for the American Revolution. Jefferson describes the virtuous disposition of the statesman that he himself practiced:

> Give up money, give up fame, give up science, and give the earth itself and all it contains rather than do an immoral act. And never suppose that in any possible situation, or under any circumstances, it is best for you to do a dishonorable thing, however slightly so it may appear to you. Whenever you are to do a thing, though it can never be known but to yourself, ask yourself how you would act were the entire world looking at you, and act accordingly. Encourage all your virtuous dispositions, and exercise them whenever an opportunity arises, being assured that they will gain strength by exercise, as a limb of the body does, and that exercise will make them habitual. From the practice of the purest virtue, you may be assured you will derive the most sublime comforts in every moment of life, and in the moment of death.[62]

Mr. Jefferson's manner was simple but dignified, and his conversational powers were of the rarest value. He was exceedingly kind and benevolent, an indulgent master to his servants, liberal and friendly to his neighbors. He possessed remarkable equanimity of temper, and it was said he was never seen in a passion. His friendship was lasting and ardent, and he was confiding

---

62 Thomas Jefferson, *Letter to His Nephew Peter Carr on August 19, 1785* (Yale Law School, Lillian Goldman Law Library).

and never distrustful. In religion, he was a free thinker; in morals, pure and unspotted; and in politics, patriotic, honest, ardent, and benevolent. His life was devoted to his country; the result of his acts in human virtue is a legacy to humankind. "I resign myself to my God and my child to my country"…these were his last words. It was a most remarkable coincidence that the twin towers of civic virtue, John Adams and Mr. Jefferson, should have died on exactly the same day on the fiftieth anniversary of that solemn act: both died on July 4, 1826, exactly fifty years after the Declaration of Independence was signed.

Jefferson was a strong supporter of the separation of church and state, believing that both government and religion would be strengthened by keeping each free of the corrupting influence of the other. In fact, the principal founding fathers (Washington, Adams, Jefferson, and Franklin) were all deeply suspicious of a European pattern of governmental involvement in religion. They saw the government as corrupting religion. Preachers who were paid by the state and paid by the government didn't pay any attention to their parishes. They didn't care about their parishioners. They brought in a hireling to do their jobs and wandered off to live somewhere else; they felt they didn't need to pay attention to their parishioners because the parishioners weren't paying them. Jefferson's general attitude toward churches, however, did not negate Jesus's teaching. In fact, he relied deeply on Jesus's teaching, thus convincing himself that the authentic words of Jesus written in the New Testament had been contaminated. He thought that early Christians, overly eager to make their religion appealing to pagans, had obscured the words of Jesus with the philosophy of the ancient Greeks and the teachings of Plato, and he commented that these "Platonists" had thoroughly muddled Jesus's original message. He thought the doctrines of Jesus to be simple and to tend to the happiness of humankind. Thomas Jefferson studied Aristotle, and he integrated many of Aristotle's concepts of society and laws into the US government and the American way of life. As a founder and statesman, Jefferson thought broadly about the virtues that need to be cultivated by policy makers in order to preserve and perfect the liberty of citizens in republican self-government. Civic virtues have historically been taught as a matter of primary concern in nations and societies under a republican form of government.

HISTORY OF REPUBLICANISM

A republic is a form of government in which the government is officially representing the people, wherein officers of state are directly or indirectly elected or appointed. In classical and medieval times, the archetype of all republics was the Roman Republic, which referred to Rome in between the period when it had kings and the periods when it had emperors. A classical republic, according to certain modern political theorists, is a state of classical antiquity that is considered to have a republican form of government—a state where sovereignty rested with the people rather than with a ruler or monarch. During the classical period, the Mediterranean region was home to several states that are now known as the classical republics, where political power was in the hands of the senate. The culture of the ancient Greeks, together with some influences from the ancient Orient, prevailed throughout classical antiquity as the basis of art, philosophy, society, and educational ideals. These ideals were preserved and imitated by the Romans. Eventually, as we recognize, the Greco-Roman cultural foundation became immensely influential on the language, politics, educational systems, philosophy, science, art, and architecture of the modern world. From the surviving fragments of the civilizations of ancient Greece and ancient Rome (classical antiquity), a revival movement was gradually formed from the fourteenth century onward, which came to be known later as the Renaissance in Western Europe, and again there was a resurgence during various neoclassical revivals in the eighteenth and nineteenth centuries.

MODERN REPUBLICANISM

The idea of modern republicanism was a creation of the Renaissance. In other words, classical republicanism (also known as civic humanism) is a form of republicanism developed in the Renaissance inspired by the governmental forms and writings of classical antiquity, especially such classical writers as Aristotle, Polybius, and Cicero. Classical republicanism is built around concepts such as civil society, civic virtue, and mixed government. During the fourteenth century, some Italian writers believed that they were experiencing the revival of great civilizations of the past because the current age showed an emphasis on artists and their achievements as it did in all great societies of the past. Scholars began comparing their accomplishments with the glories of the achievements of ancient Greece and Rome. Florentine scholar, humanist, historian, and statesman, Leonardo Bruni (1370–1444), believed that the best form of government was republican or representative. He and other like-minded thinkers found such a government when they studied ancient Rome (the Roman Republic) before the emperors came to power. They believed this was the best model for a government to take. They believed in patriotism and in humanistic learning and that the residents of Florence and other Italian cities should be proud of their heritage. This movement encouraged education in social and political life.

These political and cultural changes eventually made their way out of Italy and into other parts of Europe. The eighteenth century, also known as the Age of Enlightenment, was a time when the ideas of the Renaissance continued to grow and become more widespread. Specifically, it was a time when advancements in science led to an emphasis on the power of human reasoning. Consequently, the theory of government based upon this Renaissance study of the past became known as "classical republicanism." Another element the classical republics shared was the central importance of citizenship. Today, the term "republic" still most commonly means a system of government that derives its power from the people rather than from another basis, such as heredity or divine right.

REPUBLICAN VIRTUE

When final decisions on public matters are made by a monarch, it is the monarch's personal virtues that influence those decisions. When a broader class of people becomes the decision maker, it is then their virtues that characterize the types of decisions made. Thus, it is important for everyone in a republic society, as well as its policy makers, to build moral character for civic virtues. A person's character is the totality of his or her character traits. Some character traits can be good, bad, or somewhere in between. They can be admirable or not. Admirable character traits, however, are the marks of perfection in virtue.

According to Aristotle, a moral virtue is a disposition to act as the morally reasonable person would act and to feel emotions and desires appropriately. We are born without moral dispositions but with the capacity to acquire those dispositions. We can develop good moral dispositions and virtue through vigilant spiritual exercise, meditating on Christ's humanism and entreating God's wisdom. Saint Thomas Aquinas, who like Jefferson also followed Aristotle's virtue, said that the highest good comes from God. Accordingly, the civic virtues that can discern political good must come from spiritual virtues that were ordained by God. Thus, the concept of ideal republican society and its citizens inseparably incorporates God's wisdom and Christ's teaching of human virtue, utilizing intellect and free will to direct human society toward universal harmony.

CHRISTIAN (FUNDAMENTALISM) INFLUENCE ON REPUBLICANISM

Now in an age preoccupied with militaristic foreign policy, the blind ambition of imperialism, and the peril of national economic inequality, the twin towers of national virtue (John Adams and Jefferson) can help us to think more clearly about our most urgent national priorities in a virtuous way. Jefferson was convinced that republican government depends less on institutional arrangements and more on cultivating a virtuous spirit in the people who run the institutions. The ultimate goal of a republican society is human happiness that is equally allocated to every member in it. Unless the republican society produces such happiness, it fails God's purpose and eventually will block the civilization from flourishing. We are witnessing such degradation in America today, precipitated by twisted Christian ideology called "dominionism" that heavily contaminates the Republican ideal.

Most of the founding fathers possessed deep religious piety in a very broad and nonspecific way without affiliating themselves too closely to religious institutions. They were in many ways quite similar to those modern Christians who rather practice goodness following Christ's teaching than proclaim religiosity. Let's be reminded that God has given us intellect and free will to exercise goodness for building His kingdom on Earth, and God's ideas were conveyed through Christ to teach the human species goodness that has to be exercised through virtuous actions in public and private in order to realize the beauty of civilization. Our intellect is to be utilized to seek the truth, our free will to decide between good and evil, and our soul to comprehend the truth and good. George Washington, father of our nation, in his farewell speech to the United States in 1796, addressed the people:

> Of all the dispositions and habits which lead to political prosperity, religion and morality are indispensable supports. In vain would that man claim the tribute of patriotism who should labor to subvert these great pillars of human happiness, these firmest props of the duties of man and citizens. The mere politician, equally with the pious man, ought to respect and to cherish them. A volume could not trace all their connections with private and public. Let it simply be asked. Where is the security for property, for reputation, for life, if the sense of religious obligation deserts the oaths, which are the instruments of investigation in Courts of Justice? And let us with caution indulge the supposition that morality can be maintained without religion. Whatever may be conceded to the influence of refined education on minds of peculiar structure, reason and experience both forbid us to expect that national morality can prevail in exclusion of religious principle.[63]

Washington's religious principle was humanistic morality, which is based on Christ's teaching of goodness. He emphasized that the virtues of politicians should adhere to this sacred teaching of Christ.

Contrary to the noble beginning of American republicanism staged by the founders, the early twentieth-century movement of Christian fundamentalism transformed American republicanism into something God would not tolerate.

---

63 George Washington, "Washington's Farewell Address, 1796" (Yale Law School, Lillian Goldman Law Library, 2008).

This is a serious political problem that we all must be aware of. Christian fundamentalism arose out of British and American Protestantism in the late nineteenth and early twentieth centuries among evangelical Christians. These founders militantly asserted that the inerrancy of the Bible was essential for true Christianity. As an organized movement, it began in the 1920s within Protestant churches—especially Baptist and Presbyterian—in the United States. Fundamentalist Christianity is often intertwined with biblical literalism. Many such churches adopted a combative style and certain theological elements, such as reconstructionism, that emphasize Bible prophecy and a belief in the imminent return of Christ. According to reconstructionism, the millennial kingdom mentioned in the scripture of Revelation will be literally fulfilled at Christ's return—after which Christ will reign on Earth for a thousand years. These fundamentalists claim that secularism and liberalism ignored God's will. Fundamentalist Christianity has been building a fanatical militant base within the Republican Party (GOP), which became the main support for a right-wing domestic agenda and foreign policy. The GOP insists that people's freedom and free enterprise will be in danger if the nation does not dominate the world with military power. Although these fanatics call themselves Christians, they are no more than wolves disguised in sheep's wool.

FUNDAMENTALISM COMBATING SECULAR HUMANISM

In today's world, there are many religious fundamentalists: Christian, Muslim, Jew, Hindu, and so on. Fundamentalists in each case cling to the literal interpretation of the holy scriptures. They can become so passionate about their beliefs that they are willing to destroy or kill those who disagree with them. A five-year examination of fundamentalism by a group of scholars concluded that there are common threads among fundamentalists.[64] Unlike traditional

---

64 Peter Steinfels, "Fundamentalism: the 20th Century's Last Ideology," *New York Times*, April 6, 1993. The thirty-five political scientists, sociologists of religion and specialists in Asia, the Middle East, and Latin America gathered in Chicago in March 1993 for the final session of a five-year examination of fundamentalism.

believers, fundamentalists consciously counterattack threats of secularism and modernity—threats often identified as outsiders or enemies. These common threads run in the excessive militant postures of Christian and Muslim fundamentalists.

Fundamentalism is a strict adherence to specific theological doctrines of religious culture and usually demonstrates a strong reaction against modern theology, combined with a vigorous attack on outside threats. For instance, American dominionists believe that America is a Christian nation, and they will deny the Enlightenment roots of American democracy. They rarely respect other religions while promoting Christian religious supremacy; they believe that only their God is the true God; they believe in the biblical law of the Old Testament and see the Constitution as a vehicle for implementing biblical law into national law. Other striking resemblances between these fundamentalists outlined by the aforementioned study group included "moral dualism," which is a view of the world as sharply divided between embattled camps of good and evil, in which fundamentalists see themselves as a group elected by divine grace and set apart from others who are evil. Perhaps it never occurred to them that only thing that can set them apart from evil is virtue, not religiosity. So far, none of these fundamentalists have demonstrated any virtue whatsoever.

Some scholars say that the "Abrahamic" forms of fundamentalism—Jewish, Christian, and Muslim—constantly affirm the absolute truth of a sacred text or authoritative tradition. These fundamentalists also emphasize messianic or millennial beliefs in a miraculous culmination of history, with Christ reigning triumphantly. No doubt fundamentalism is off mainstream society. Whether it's Muslim or Christian fundamentalism, religious extremists damage their religions and societies. In the middle of the twentieth century, some naïvely believed that secularism was the coming ideology and that religion would never again play an important role in world affairs. But where warfare is endemic as it is in the Middle East, fundamentalists participate in the violence that pervades the entire region. They have staged revolutions, assassinated their national leaders, carried out terrorist atrocities, and become an influential political force that menaces international peace.

American fundamentalism, synonymous with dominionism, is a different form of subversive force, attempting to influence national policy making by highlighting dominion ideology. It wages war, on one hand, against modern secular society, the liberal philosophy of Democrats, and against the evil force of Muslim terrorists on the other hand. Their aggressive military buildup is aimed at protecting the nation against so-called evil forces. American fundamentalists want Christian government, however, wrongly they define it to be. There is no doubt that in Saudi Arabia, the United Arab Emirates, Israel, and the United States, fundamentalists are dominating foreign policy. It's not surprising that among all these aggressive military nations, the United States is the most dominant power, with 43 percent of the entire world's military power and spending 32 percent ($696 billion) of the national revenue in 2011.[65]

The undercurrent of any fundamentalist movement, whether Judaism, Christianity, or Islam, is the belief that modern secular humanism is the major danger to their religion. Secular humanism is a naturalistic philosophy that holds the idea of ethics as consequential—that is, to be judged by results. This is in contrast to so-called "commanded" ethics, in which right and wrong are defined in advance and attributed to divine authority. Secular humanism and its underlying argument claim that nature (the world of everyday physical experience) is all there is and that reliable knowledge is best obtained when we query nature using the scientific method. Hence, secular humanism demands a total commitment to the use of critical reason, factual evidence, and scientific methods of inquiry, rather than faith and mysticism, in seeking solutions to human problems and answers to important human questions. The term originally referred to a Renaissance spirit, with its emphasis on secular studies (the humanities), in rejection of medieval religious authority. The Renaissance is best described by the word "humanism," which was a cultural and intellectual movement that emphasized secular ideas as a result of the rediscovery and

---

65 Source: The Center for Arms Control and Non-Proliferation. The Center for Arms Control and Non-Proliferation is a national nonpartisan, nonprofit dedicated to enhancing peace and security through expert policy analysis and thought-provoking research. Its affiliated organization is the Council for a Livable World, founded in 1962 by Leo Szilard. For more than fifty years, the Council for a Livable World has been advocating for a more principled approach to US-national security and foreign policy.

study of the literature, art, and civilization of ancient Greece and Rome. In its modern usage, humanism often indicates a general emphasis on scientific knowledge, lasting human values, and human morality.

FUNDAMENTALISM CONTRADICTS MORAL VALUE OF HUMANISM

Modern humanists are committed to science as the best method for constructing knowledge and testing its reliability. Humanists recognize the distinctiveness of the human species as the only animal so far to have developed critical consciousness and culture. Humanists believe that we humans are the only species thus far to have evolved with the intellectual capacity to construct reliable knowledge of our surroundings and about ourselves. Another aspect of human distinctiveness is creative capacity. Thus, humanists cherish all the magnificent creations that have enriched world civilization throughout the centuries. They cherish modern civilization, not because they are inspired by some transcending spirit, but as the products of our remarkable human imagination. Humanism focuses particularly on the significance of an aspect of human distinctiveness: humankind's capacity for morality. By this, they mean human "intellect" (to acquire values, to create ideals, and to make choices), which then functions to direct and shape individual characters and therefore, ultimately, provides direction to the very culture that gave them birth.

Although ethics or morality is shared by every theological and philosophical system of thought, humanists differ from all the others in that their beliefs are grounded in the totality of the experience of the human race, from time immemorial. Humanists trust human intellect in making choices that contributes to personal fulfillment for individuals and the society of which they are an integral part. They believe, through rational conclusion, that humans can select criteria that can establish rules for justice, kindness, and peacefulness in human affairs. In modern societies, most liberal ideals are intimately connected to this humanism philosophy.

Fundamentalism is not going to disappear or retreat to the sidelines and confine itself to private life unless human virtue is taught to these fundamentalists by their own virtuous leaders, who can subdue their aggressive activities by countering them with good. Unfortunately, we have to take fundamentalism very seriously at the present time. This religious ideology has taken over the Republican Party and turned the country into an aggressive nation as the ruling empire of the twenty-first century. Protestant fundamentalists feel that liberals despise them, and this has resulted in a fundamentalism that has gone way beyond Jerry Falwell and the Moral Majority of the 1970s. The Moral Majority was formally initiated as a result of a struggle for control of an American conservative Christian-advocacy group known as the Christian Voice in 1978. During a 1979 meeting, they urged televangelist Jerry Falwell to found Moral Majority. This was also the beginning of the New Christian Right.

Dominionism is a term used to describe the tendency among some politically active conservative Christians to seek influence or control over secular civil government through political action, with the goal of a nation governed by conservative Christians, or fundamentalists. Now, one may think that dominionists are too small a group to be dangerous. But it only takes a small percentage of people who wield the power of wealth and influence to change the course of politics and national destiny. These individuals may be a small handful of Christians, but there is a very large Christian population that makes up 85 percent of the nation. These Christians create a climate where religious talk in politics is welcome and maybe even somewhat encouraged so that dominionists can pander to the religious sensibilities of these Christians. For example, they can undermine gay-marriage rights or contraceptive issues by citing religious reasons that a large percentage of Christians might support because of moral issues. They can attack abortion rights and women's rights, and continually attack perceived moral issues based on religious belief. They can also whip up the religious base into a fury over perceived slights. If dominionists can convince the majority of Christians that their religion is under attack, it will be easier for them to enforce legislation favoring such pseudo-Christian belief. There is no doubt that such un-Christian zealotry is a religious and political pathology that not only smears good Christian community but also threatens nation's destiny.

FUNDAMENTALISTS' CONCEPT OF WEALTH AND POVERTY

Dominionists inherently believe that wealth in itself indicates God's approval of men and nations, whereas poverty and sickness reflect God's disapproval. The idea comes from twisting the interpretation of passages in Deuteronomy in the Old Testament. Using the text of Deuteronomy 28, which is a list of God's blessings and curses, Pat Robertson (host of The 700 Club) and other dominionists claim that the book reveals God's covenant in economic law: that God only bestows material wealth or blessings upon those who are among his elect and that God does so because these are the individuals and nations who obey his commandments and laws. With this kind of tunnel-vision orthodoxy, it is not so surprising to see that these people tend to value the protection of the wealthy, turning their cheeks away from the poor. According to dominionists, the poor and wretched are products of God's curse. Thus, according to these zealots, an attempt to lift the poor out of poverty or save people from poverty and ill health violates the will of almighty God. Taking it one step further, if this is God's attitude toward the poor, then it's morally wrong to help them. So it's easy to see how social security and Medicare are viewed by dominionists as evil programs that rob money from good citizens to enrich the wretched.

To illustrate the gloomy picture of poverty, which has been neglected by the US government for so long, I want to draw your attention to American people living with disabilities who receive supplemental security ;income (SSI) payments. They continue to be the nation's poorest citizens. Are these people products of God's curse? In 2010, the annual income of a single individual receiving SSI payments was $8,436, equal to only 18.7 percent of the national median income for a one-person household and over 20 percent below the 2010 federal poverty level of $10,830. Since the first "Priced Out" study was published in 1998 by Technical Assistance Collaborative, Inc., SSI payments relative to median income have declined precipitously—from 24.4 percent of the median income in 1998 to 18.7 percent in 2010—while national average rents have risen over 50 percent during the same time frame. In 2010, as a national average, a person receiving SSI needed to pay 112 percent of his or her monthly receipts to rent a modest one-bedroom unit. In twelve years, the amount of monthly SSI income needed to rent that modest one bedroom unit has increased 62 percent. Hence, people with disabilities are even priced out of the smallest studio/efficiency units, which averaged 99 percent of monthly SSI payments.

In 2010, although twenty-one states provided discretionary state-SSI supplements to people living independently in the community, these supplements had little impact on the housing-affordability crisis experienced by people living with disabilities. Even in Alaska (which had the highest state-SSI supplement of $362 and a total monthly SSI payment of $1,036), people living with disabilities receiving SSI still needed to pay over 80 percent of their monthly income to rent a modest one-bedroom unit. The Republican-controlled US Congress has not lifted a finger to mend such problems, shifting the responsibility to states instead. The dominionists believe that those who are poor, sick, and weak are so situated because God's wrath has been visited upon them. Here is a sample from Deuteronomy 28, which is frequently cited by dominionists:

> The Lord shall cause thee to be smitten before thine enemies... thy carcass shall be food unto all fowls of the air...The Lord will smite thee with boils, tumors, and with the scab, and with the itch, whereof thou canst not be healed. The Lord shall smite thee with madness and blindness and astonishment of heart; thou shalt grope at noonday; thou shalt not prosper in thy ways; and thou shalt be only oppressed and spoiled evermore...thou shalt betroth a wife and another man shall lie with her; thou shalt build an house, and thou shalt not dwell therein, and thine ox shall be slain before thine eyes, and thou shalt not eat thereof; thine ass shall be violently taken away from before thy face and shall not be restored to thee; thy sheep shall be given unto thine enemies, and thou shalt have none to rescue them. Thy sons and thy daughters shall be given unto another people, and thine eyes shall look, and fail with longing for

them all the day long; and there shall be no might in thine hand. The fruit of thy land, and all thy labors, shall a nation whom thou knowest not eat up, and thou shalt be only oppressed and crushed always.

One must understand the full meaning of Deuteronomy 28 in relation to entire context of the biblical book. Moses, who may well be a mythical figure, tells his people, the Israelites, how to make a success of their life as a people once they are settled in the land. The choice presented to Israelites is to worship a single deity, Yahweh, and keep his commandments, or to serve other gods and be condemned. Previous to Moses's time, the Israelites had been polytheists, particularly serving Baalim (Baal). Moses, coming out of wilderness, had come into contact with Baal worshipers, who were shouting to Baal and dancing around the altar and, in their frenzied excitement, cut themselves with knives and lancets till they were all covered with blood. (Baal is the male principal of life and reproduction in nature and as such is sometimes honored by acts of the foulest sensuality, including sacrifices of oxen and other animals being offered up to Baal, and also children of both sexes frequently being burned in sacrifice.) In the face of such shamanistic brutality and licentious immorality, only forceful threat would convince these uncivilized, uncouth earthlings who understood at least what survival means. Deuteronomy 28 was addressed precisely to Moses's flock, who had quickly been sucked into such foul worship. So it appears that Moses gave them a choice that would determine what kind of life they would make for themselves in the land. Whichever choice they made as a people carried consequences, which Deuteronomy terms "blessing" and "curse." Thus, the book can be deemed as a survival manual for Israel as it contains a tone of life-or-death urgency. Deuteronomy, along with the books of Joshua, Judges, Samuel, and Kings, presents biblical story of Israel from Moses to the time of the Babylonian exile. Hence, the book of Deuteronomy is important to Judaism, while Christians are expected to maintain a relationship with God through Christ's teachings of humanism. If Republican dominionists expect Christians to consent to the underlying statement cited in Deuteronomy 28 as a sacred law of God—condemning public welfare and government assistance—they are indeed vicious fools, not Christians.

In contrast to the US Republican's "ungodly" welfare philosophy, our good neighbor, the Canadian government, has been engaged in a campaign to end poverty. The Canadian National Council of Welfare concluded, after three years of research and observation, that elimination of national poverty benefits everyone. (According to an OECD report, the relative poverty rate in Canada was 11.9 percent, compared to the United States with 17.4 percent in 2012.) Canada provides a special widows' benefit to assist elderly women living alone (who compose the largest single-poverty group), whereas the United States has no such program. Canada's social-welfare programs are much more generous than those in the United States in several areas where such generosity is particularly helpful in reducing poverty. For instance, unlike Aid to Families with Dependent Children(AFDC)—the US federal-assistance program in effect from 1935 to 1996, created by the Social Security Act and administered by the United States Department of Health and Human Services to provide financial assistance to children of single parents or whose families had low or no income—Canada's principal means-tested social program, "social assistance," is available to individuals and couples even without children, and the benefit levels are substantially higher. In contrast to the US Earned Income Tax Credit, Canada's child tax benefit is available not just to working families, but to nonworking ones as well. Canada provides a guaranteed-income supplement to the elderly, which ensures that elderly individuals and couples have an income no less than 55–60 percent of the nation's median, while American retirees' average receipt of social-security income is less than 25 percent of the national median income. A study released by the National Academy of Social Insurance (NASI) in 2007 states that the US average social-security benefit is only about $1,000 a month for retired workers, which puts them at the poverty level until they die. A new SSA report as of January 2015 shows $1,285 a month—a small increase in eight years. As one can see clearly, these recipients are put into the twilight zone instead of enjoying the sunset of life in comfort.

Most of the ten poorest states in America are dominated by Republican Party, not because Republican candidates are representing the poor but because they are predominantly Christian. Mississippi is the poorest with a poverty rate of 21.5 percent, followed by New Mexico, Louisiana, Alabama, Kentucky, Arkansas, Tennessee, West Virginia, Georgia, Arizona, and South Carolina.[66] Most of these states are in what we call the Bible belt, which means people in these regions are very much Christians, believing in every word of the Bible. Thus, it is easy for the Republican Party to win over them using principles of Christian morality. Obviously, this means that even poor people have enough sense to vote for the traditional values of Christianity, not understanding fully what they mean to them. For instance, they oppose tax hikes, which does not in any way help these poor folks get out of their poverty status. In fact, there is no mention of eliminating poverty in the Republican platform other than preserving all defense options to defend the nation. As it reads: "All Americans should affirm that our first obligation is the security of our country. To all those who defend it, we owe our full support and gratitude."

REPUBLICAN PARTY PLATFORM AND MILITARY BUILDUP

The Republican platform extensively covers national security—the current conflict abroad, homeland security, terrorism and nuclear proliferation, fighting bioterrorism and cyberterrorism, providing for the armed forces, and so on—as the foremost government responsibility in securing the peace of nation. Accordingly, they justify the total defense-related spending of $878.5 billion in 2011, comprising military defense, civil defense, veteran support, foreign-military aid, and foreign-economic aid. It should be noted that the frequently quoted $696 billion for military expenditure is only a partial amount of national defense spending in 2011. The total national defense spending can be translated into 40 percent of national revenue received in 2011 ($2,174 trillion). In the same year, the nation suffered a budget deficit of $1.3 trillion.

---

66 The US Census Bureau, Income, Poverty and Health Insurance Coverage in the United States, 2014.

Anyone can guess where this huge deficit came from. Yet the Republican Party often blames the Democratic administration as reckless big spenders. The Republicans specifically accused President Obama's $800 billion stimulus package as wasted money and a failure when the federal government was broke. On the contrary, many economists argued at the time that the stimulus should have been a lot bigger and criticized that the Obama administration should have shown more backbone by demanding more. I might add that the president has yet to show strong backbone in cutting the national-defense budget to a minimal level and shifting the future-defense budget to the battlefield of fighting against the poverty of this nation.

Remember that classical republicanism, tracing back to ancient Greece, emphasized none other than protection of common welfare for citizens as the primary characteristic of good government. And republican government, as the founders of America insisted, was the only kind of government that can offer this protection. So they confidently elected a "republic" as the American way of life over two hundred years ago. Reviewing the civic virtue of the Republican Party today, however, one cannot erase the dismal picture of the national economy tilting toward the protection of the rich, where the livelihood of the working people is unprotected.

America's unions have been a backbone element of the New Deal coalition since President Franklin Roosevelt signed the legislation into law on July 5, 1935, to legally recognize unions as representatives of workers in many industries in the United States. They have been able to engage in collective bargaining for better terms and conditions at work and take collective action, including strike if necessary. But the Republicans have consistently wanted to break all unions apart, especially the teachers' union— while claiming that their goal is to achieve the kingdom of God. By the 1970s, rapidly increasing imports had begun to undercut American producers, while many corporations moved their factories offshore to low-wage countries. Republicans, using conservative think tanks, began to push through legislative process to curb the power of public employee unions as well as eliminate business regulations. Numerous industries were deregulated, including airlines, trucking, railroads, and telephones, over the objections of the unions involved. Hence, union membership among workers in private industry shrank dramatically, coupled with deregulation and free competition.

For Republican dominionists, liberals who want to redistribute the wealth to the poor and needy, who desire the welfare and happiness of all Americans, who insists on safety regulations for citizens' protection, and who desire the preservation of American values are all noisy secular humanists who must be reduced to powerlessness. The dominionistic Republican vision of world peace is:

> Through strength requires a sustained international effort, which complements our military activities, to develop and maintain alliances and relationships that will lead to greater peace and stability... To be successful international leaders, we must uphold international law, including the laws of war, and update them when necessary. Our moral standing requires that we respect what are essentially American principles of justice. In any war of ideas, our values will triumph.[67]

Dominionists teach that all nations should convert to biblical laws (Old Testament laws), which are superior to secular laws. Therefore, Christians must be willing to overthrow all secular laws. In other words, a measure of one's spirituality rests upon one's willingness to take dominion over not only the people of America but also the entire world. Under dominionism, any lawful government ordained by God can execute retribution and punishment upon those who challenge the government's unjust policies. When read this way, it takes on a new and sinister meaning. Or it can be read to mean that once a new government of the United States of America has been established under biblical law, then no citizen will have the right to resist it or rebel against its laws. The Declaration of Independence will no longer be applicable to the dominionists.

In the eras of the fifties and sixties, people worried about communism taking over the world. Along with communism, another enemy to Christianity was identified recently by dominionists. This enemy is nothing

---

67 2008 Republican Party Platform.

other than secular humanism. In 1982, Francis Schaeffer, who was then the leading evangelical theologian, called secular humanism the greatest threat to Christianity the world had ever seen. To dominionists, secular humanism, like communism, is based on atheism, which was sufficient enough for Schaeffer to conclude that humanism was an enemy to the kingdom of God. Probably, it never occurred to him why these gentle humanists turned their back against Christianity, if they ever did.

REPUBLICAN'S CRIMINAL JUSTICE

According to dominionists, every person must submit to governing authorities, since the existing authorities are instituted by God. Consequently, anyone who rebels against authority is resisting a divine institution, and those who so resist have himself or herself to thank for the punishment he or she will receive. You wish to have no fear of the authorities? Then continue to do right, and you will have their approval, for they are God's agents working for your good. But if you are doing wrong, then you will have cause to fear them, as it is not for nothing that they hold the power of the sword, for they are God's agents of punishment, for retribution on the offender. That is why you are obliged to submit. It is an obligation imposed not merely by fear of retribution but by conscience. The authorities are in God's service, and to these duties they devote their energies. The Republican platform clearly states this policy on offenders:

> Locking Up Criminals—Criminals behind bars cannot harm the general public…Individuals, including juveniles, who are repeat offenders or who commit serious crimes need to be prosecuted and punished. Reviews of death sentences imposed for murdering a police officer should be expedited.

It's no wonder why prisons and jails are crowded by a steep increase in inmates in excess of five times more in 2010 than 1980. (See figure 13 in chapter 11,

"Consequences of Inequality.") Such is the Republican punitive criminal justice and policy, designed more to allay fear than reduce crime. The United States has less than 5 percent of the world's population, but it has almost 25 percent of the world's prisoners. According to a US Department of Justice report released in December 2011, 47 percent of sentenced prisoners in state prisons at year end 2008 were in for nonviolent or nonserious transgressions. In addition to the state- or federal-run prison population, the average daily jail population in locally operated places (usually county-run facilities) was 776,573 in 2008. Of these convicted jail inmates, 39 percent were nonserious convicts. In terms of costs, America spent $60 billion collectively on state and local correction facilities, which translates to taxpayers paying $23,000 a year to house and feed each prisoner.

In 2008, the United States had 2.3 million criminals behind bars, more than any other nation, according to data maintained by the International Center for Prison Studies at King's College, London. It had 751 people in prison or jail for every 100,000 in the population. The only other major industrialized nation that even comes close is Russia, with 627 prisoners for every 100,000 people. Other countries have much lower rates. For instance, England's rate is 151; Europe's average is 100 and Japan's is 63. Prison sentences here in the United States have become much harsher than in any other country in the world. Vivien Stern, a research fellow at the Prison Studies Center in London, said that the American incarceration rate has made the United States "a rogue state," a country that has made a decision not to follow what is a normal Western approach. For instance, "life sentence" means a prison term of around fifteen years in Denmark, Finland, and Sweden, and Norway has abolished life sentences altogether and replaced it with a twenty-one-year maximum term. In the United States, life sentence means *life* without the possibility of parole. In Europe, imprisonment is used only for more serious offenses, and the majority of penalties imposed consist of less severe alternatives, such as community work or unpaid work. There is no death penalty in Europe. In fact, Europe today is the only region in the world where the death penalty is no longer applied. All the Council of Europe's forty seven member states have either abolished capital punishment or instituted a moratorium on executions. European prisons are without walls: the prisoner is obliged to stay in the prison area, but there are no guards or fences.

As we can see, the American justice system is established under the influence of dominionistic Republicans, emphasizing more strongly the punishment of offenders rather than the protection of citizens' welfare. Most crimes are associated with helpless poor people with poor economic backgrounds who have few options in life. In many cases, those who've been incarcerated grew up around family members and friends who suffered the same fate. Their ability to escape the poverty pit decreases greatly after their first offense, as their earnings are almost slashed in half because many employers refuse to hire them. The most unsettling fact is that more than half of those incarcerated were the primary financial providers for their children. One in every twenty eight children in America had an incarcerated parent in 2010. Compare that to this statistic: that one in every 125 children had an incarcerated parent a quarter of a century ago. This rise, of course, can be attributed to the implementation of harsher laws for lesser crimes—two-thirds of today's incarcerated parents committed nonviolent offenses. Such reality is very serious because children's chances of growing up as productive, law-abiding, and happy adults are greatly diminished when their parents are not able to protect and lead them in their life. The nation's growing prison-and-jail population is raising serious questions about the collateral effects on children, families, and communities. Needless to say, imprisonment disrupts positive, nurturing relationships between parents—particularly mothers—and their children. In addition, many families with children suffer economic strain and instability when a parent is imprisoned.

All of the aforementioned facts and discussions explain how distorted the notion of God's law actually is, as it's been put into practice by the American Republic in recent decades. This stems from none other than the dominionists' fanatic ideology. No virtuous republican nation would allow such destructive elements—militant, uncompassionate, and punitive government policies—that shackle citizens' freedom and happiness. The American value of "maintaining the sanctity and dignity of human life" cannot be actualized by itself without policy makers restoring their civic virtues, which were strongly emphasized by the founding fathers of the nation. Those honorable founding fathers stand as contemporary models for American republicanism. They are the embodiment of the liberal soul in the body of republicanism, which is what American Republicans should practice.

Chapter 8

AMERICAN CAPITALISM

PURITANISM IN AMERICA

People from Europe came to America searching for religious freedom, escaping the religious persecution they faced in their home countries. They had dreams and visions for a bright future in the New World. The Puritans were men and women out on this mission, and they became nation builders. When we examine history, their source of inspiration was the Word of God. No doubt the Puritans played a big part in the settlement of America, and they were also very influential in the American Revolution, along with Enlightenment thinkers.

The eighteenth century is often called the Age of Enlightenment because it was characterized by scientific rationality, self-critical awareness, ever-improving technology, democracy, religious tolerance, universal peace, and the continuing improvement of people's lives, both in terms of physical comfort and intellectual expansion. The Age of Enlightenment opened a new chapter of human history by closing the old history of general ignorance and backwardness of a population that had been kept in the dark by religious authorities for many centuries. Slavery was abolished; torture and cruel punishment were removed from judicial systems, and freedom of conscience was heralded by the separation of church and state. Progress was the banner under which these enlightened thinkers decided to abandon old ways and move into a brighter future. Optimism and faith in the basic goodness of human beings were typical dispositions of Enlightenment thinkers.

These men of enlightenment unequivocally did play a big part in the early formation of America alongside the Puritans. But the Puritan dream was loftier than that of the Enlightenment thinkers. Those Puritans wanted to build a nation reflecting the glory of God. It would be a kingdom of God that this world had never seen before. Not only would it be governed in a rational way, reflecting Christian principles, but also their governmental proceedings would be conducted under the spirit of God they'd learned from the Bible. They believed that America under the favor of God would become a blessed and prosperous nation. The nation would become the light to the world, a shining city upon a hill.

Without a doubt, the Protestant ethic influenced large numbers of American people to engage in businesses of the secular world, developing their own enterprises and accumulating wealth. According to the new Protestant religion, an individual was religiously compelled to follow a secular vocation with as much zeal as possible. Thus, the Protestant work ethic, self-reliance and hard work, was an important force behind the development of capitalism, and it became the central strand for the fabric of American ideals. The Protestants forbade the wasteful use of hard-earned money by donating to the poor or to welfare programs, since such a condition was caused by laziness and thus an offense to God. The same ideas still pervade Christian conservative and Republican thought today.

THE BEGINNING OF AMERICAN CAPITALISM

Between 1865 and 1920, the United States became the world's dominant economic, industrial, and agricultural power. This period is frequently referred to by historians as the age of big business, whose interests were served on all levels of government. The powerful, new business groups exerted extraordinary influence on state and local governments, and local taxes were unreasonably light on the largest enterprises. After the end of Reconstruction in 1877, the legislature enacted numerous regressive taxes, including a general-property tax that bore most heavily on small property holders. For example, almost every piece of property owned by blacks, however insignificant, was taxed.

In addition, in North Carolina, for instance, industrial and agricultural capitalists consorted to strip the poor of their political rights. The issue of voting rights in the United States has been much contested throughout its history. Eligibility to vote in the United States is established both in the US Constitution and its amendments, and by state law. But in the absence of a specific federal law or constitutional provision, each state is given considerable discretion to establish qualifications for suffrage and candidacy within its own respective jurisdiction. Hence, the state-constitutional provisions, as well as election laws, were rewritten to deprive both the poor and blacks of their vote. As the poor lost their vote, they also were saddled with unequal schooling taxes. Blacks paid higher taxes for education than did white (and poor whites paid higher taxes than rich whites.) In addition to this heavy tax burden on the poor blacks, the gap between per capita expenditures allocated for the education of blacks and of whites widened steadily in the coming years, and there was increasing inequality between the rich and poor after 1900.

More than any other period in history, the Industrial Revolution clearly divided between the rich and the poor, the haves and the have-nots. By creating an inevitable dependency of masses of poor people on employers who give them wages, capitalism was thus firmly established as the dominant economic system that we still live under today. As industrialization expanded and bloomed, companies got larger, with a growing separation between the workers and owners. The rise of these large firms is what really developed the labor based capitalist system during the Industrial Revolution.

With the purchasing power that came with employment, the hitherto poor now became the major consumers, while the large businesses profited big, and thus capitalism expanded. People began to buy things from those businesses that employed them. Of course, such a cycle is sustainable when the wealth distribution is well balanced. In reality, it was obvious in the burgeoning industrialization of the nineteenth century that the division between the wealthy and poor, the powerful and powerless, was being distinctly defined with lopsided wealth distribution.

DARWINISM INTO CAPITALISM

The Darwinian world view was critical not only in influencing the development of Nazism and communism but also in the rise of the ruthless capitalism that began to flourish in the late 1800s and early 1900s. A key aspect of this brand of capitalism was its extreme individualism, which indicated that other people counted for little and that it is both natural and proper to exploit the weaker. The so-called robber barons often claimed that their behavior was justified by natural law[68] and was the inevitable outcome of human history. Many of these barons were raised as Christians but rejected their Christianity or modified it to include Darwinian ideas. For example, Andrew Carnegie (1835–1919) once accepted Christianity but abandoned it for Darwinism and became a friend of social Darwinist Herbert Spencer (1820–1903). The Darwinian concept, applied to business, still is very much with us today. The "survival of the fittest" theory in biology was quickly interpreted by capitalists as an ethical precept that sanctioned cutthroat economic competition. Julian Huxley and H. B. D. Kittlewell in their book, *Charles Darwin and His World*, concluded that social Darwinism led to the glorification of free enterprise, laissez-faire economics, and war.

Social Darwinism undoubtedly was adopted in defense of competitive individualism and laissez-faire capitalism in England and in America. In keeping with Darwinian principles, business either swallows the competition or is swallowed by that competition. Darwin's ideas, specifically the social Darwinism of Hebert Spencer known as "survival of the fittest," played a

---

68 Natural law or the law of nature is a system of law that is purportedly determined by nature and thus universal. Classically, natural law refers to the use of reason to analyze human nature—both social and personal—and deduce binding rules of moral behavior. According to natural law theory, which holds that morality is a function of human nature and reason can discover valid moral principles by looking at the nature of humanity in society, the content of positive law (man-made law) cannot be known without some reference to natural law. Some use natural law synonymously with natural justice or natural right. Although natural law is often conflated with common law, the two are distinct in that natural law is a view that certain rights or values are inherent in or universally cognizable by virtue of human reason or human nature, while common law is the legal tradition whereby certain rights or values are legally cognizable by virtue of judicial recognition or articulation. Natural law theories have, however, exercised a profound influence on the development of English common law and have featured greatly in the philosophies of Thomas Aquinas, John Locke, and so many others (https://en.wikipedia.org/wiki/Natural_law).

critically important role in the development and growth not only of Nazism and communism but also of the ruthless form of capitalism as best illustrated by the robber barons. "Robber baron" is a term used for a powerful nineteenth-century American businessman. By the 1890s, the term was typically applied to businessmen who were viewed as having used questionable practices to amass their wealth. It combines the sense of criminal ("robber") and illegitimate aristocracy ("baron"). Simply, "survival of the fittest" implies that the strong will succeed, and the weak will perish. The "fittest" will be successful, and they shall rule the weaker because they are the most fit to do so. In a brutal world without social hierarchy, class, and social customs, this would mean that the person who is the strongest with a large amount of capital rules over everyone. So the idea of the "fittest" became the social mores highly acceptable in America. The leaders of the capitalistic world (the Rockefellers, the Carnegies, and many other industrialists) took hold of this idea to justify their entrepreneurial behaviors. Social Darwinism is the application of what was interpreted as the law of evolution, in which those who succeed in society were superior to those who did not succeed. In the minds of the radical social Darwinist, to be successful and ruthless at business was no different than an animal eating other animals for food. To them, it is how the human world operates.

This concept originated with Spencer during the late 1800s. He based his ideas on the findings of scientist Charles Darwin, who developed the theory of evolution that species improved over time with the strongest triumphing over the weak. Applying evolutionary theory to society, Spencer concluded that some people were destined for wealth and power because they were naturally stronger, and the stronger members of society would triumph over the weaker members. Inevitably in a capitalist society, those weaker members are the people who occupy the lowest social strata—those in poverty. Capitalists argue that governments should not interfere with competition by attempting to regulate the economy or cure social ills such as poverty. Social Darwinism provided wealthy and powerful people with a justification for their existence, and some proponents of social Darwinism preposterously believed that God ordained certain people to be wealthy and live comfortably on the hard work of others. John. D. Rockefeller (1839–1937), president of the Standard Oil Company, once contended that "the growth of a large business is merely a survival of the fittest." It is important to understand the belief perceived by these defenders: To them, capitalism is a moral system because it is dedicated to the protection of rights—right to life, right to liberty, right to property, and right to the pursuit of happiness—which is a requirement for human survival and flourishing. It is the only system that safeguards the freedom of the individual and recognizes the sanctity of the human rights, and capitalism creates a political and economic system that permits the greatest possibility for self-determination and moral agency. They defended capitalism vigorously on a narrowly defined moral basis of rights and freedom, rather than a utilitarian basis. In utilitarianism, everything is useful if it creates happiness. However, an action must be judged for its consequences on the happiness of the largest number. That is, one's action for pursuit of happiness must be curtailed if it decreases the happiness of the largest number of the society. Also, personal freedom must be weighed in light of the freedom of other individuals and of the community. In other words, one's freedom must be checked when it hinders or diminishes the freedom of another individual or the well-being of the society.

No doubt, social Darwinism gave capitalists legitimate social power, allowing them to assume moral authority and to a large degree influence political decisions to their benefit without heeding the massive poor population in the society they live in. The real problem arises when the size of global population growth reaches an unbearable level, and material resources become severely limited. There is only so much land (and other resources) to go around. One's amassment of wealth encroaching on what somebody else should get will create conflict in the society between the haves and have-nots, as those who lose out resent those who possess more than an equitable share of wealth. The outcome of unrestrained freedom of capitalists is undoubtedly detrimental to human society in violation of the universal law of harmony— divine proportion.

Chapter 9

THE US WEALTH DISTRIBUTION

In 2012, the top 1 percent of Americans controlled 42 percent of the national wealth, while the bottom 90 percent collectively owns just 23 percent of total U.S. wealth, about as much as in 1940.[69] Between 1979 and 2007, average after-tax incomes for the top 1 percent rose by 281 percent after adjusting for inflation compared to increases of 48 percent for the bottom 20 percent households.[70] Another incredible fact is that the wealthiest 400 Americans' accumulation is equal to the combined wealth of bottom 61 percent of the country combined—a staggering 194 million people.[71] No matter how you slice it, when it comes to income and wealth in America, the rich group gets most of the pie, and the rest get the leftovers. That is, in the United States wealth is highly concentrated in relatively few hands.

---

69 Source: PATHWAYS • *The Poverty and Inequality Report 2016*, The Stanford Center on Poverty and Inequality.

70 Data from the Center on Budget and Policies, October 26, 2015

71 Source: Institute for Policy Studies, *Billionaire Bonanza: The Forbes 400 and the Rest of Us*, December 1, 2015

REAGANOMICS AND TRICKLE-DOWN ECONOMIC POLICY

The wealth and income of the rich began to accumulate mostly starting in 1981, at the beginning of Reagan's presidency. Supply-side economics is the cornerstone of Republican belief that has driven US economic policy since the Reagan presidency (better known as "Reaganomics," or "trickle-down" policy).[72] Under this economic theory, greater tax cuts for rich investors and entrepreneurs, as incentives to save and reinvest in production, is stressed. The supply siders believe that producers (mega corporations) and their willingness to create more goods and services will trigger economic growth expressed in the GDP. On the question of regulatory policy, supply siders tend to ally with traditional political conservatives, or Republicans—those who would prefer a smaller government and less intervention in free-market activities.

Supply-side economics presupposes that production or supply is the key to economic prosperity and that consumption by citizens or demand is merely a secondary consequence. In other words, if government economic policy focuses on helping the business (mega corporations) in their productions, the benefits will "trickle-down" to general consumers. In reality, the past thirty years of Republican economics has proven that the trickle-down theory cripples national prosperity, favoring the rich with the benefits trickling *up* to make the very wealthy even wealthier. It is evident how little growth has trickled down to typical American families under supply-side economics. Over this period, rich Americans' incomes relentlessly kept growing, with Republican protection lowering taxes along with deregulation of financial-market activities while the rest

---

72 Supply-side economics as macroeconomic theory argues that economic growth can be most effectively created by lowering barriers for people to produce (supply) goods and services, such as lowering income-tax and capital gains–tax rates, and by allowing greater flexibility by reducing regulation. According to supply-side economics, consumers will then benefit from a greater supply of goods and services at lower prices. Typical policy recommendations of supply-side economists are lower marginal-tax rates and less regulation. Proponents argue that lowering taxes for people, especially for those who have a lot of money to invest, will always lead to better economic results. Supply-side economics is frequently cited as "trickle-down economics" (Source: Wikipedia, the free encyclopedia). Also see Reaganomics at http://www.ushistory.org/us/59b.asp.

of the Americans became poorer. To top it all, the supply siders turned the United States into a debt-ridden nation (that continues to this day to see shrinking national revenue) by lowering taxes to mega-rich corporations and rich individuals.

In the fiscal year 2010, the federal government spent $3.5 trillion. Of that amount, only $2.2 trillion was financed by federal tax revenues (including the social security trust fund). The remaining $1.3 trillion was financed by borrowing. This deficit will ultimately have to be paid for by future taxpayers. Mr. Buffett said the mega rich in America pay income taxes at a rate of about 15 percent on most of their earnings, while the majority of Americans with below $100,000 annual earnings paid closer to 19 percent.[73]

As of today, the Republican Congress continually supports tax cuts for the rich, especially for corporations, insisting that the best way to stimulate national economic growth is by protecting large corporations. Consequently, corporate-income tax collected in 2010 was only 9 percent of government revenue. Since the rise of Reaganomics three decades ago, the government has succumbed to crony capitalism backing the wealthy. As a result, a large share of the nation's economic growth over the past thirty years has gone to the top rich people who operate mega corporations. This is a dismal fact. About 46.2 million people live in dire poverty, according to the 2010 Census Bureau report—the highest number since the government began tracking poverty in 1959. For a family of four with two children, poverty means making less than $22,113 a year.

As more income has been pushed to the top small number of rich people over the past thirty years, the income growth of America's middle class has not kept pace with the growth of the economy. In fact, 80 percent of America has gone down almost $10,000 per year in income growth since 1979, while the top 1 percent is up over $740,000 in average income, according to the

---

73 Warren E. Buffet, "*Stop Coddlin g the Super-Rich*" New York Times, August 14, 2011.

Center on Budget and Policy Priorities (CBPP).[74] In an economy that depends on 70 percent personal consumption, such economic weakness of the majority of the population, including the middle class, will continually weaken the demand for goods and services and thus slow national economic growth and spurn higher unemployment. Back in May 2011, a report by the OECD stated that the gap between the rich and poor in OECD countries (most of which are high-income economies) had reached its highest level in over thirty years, and governments had to act quickly to tackle this ominous inequality.

In May 2015, OECD Secretary-General addressed again the seriousness of inequality by saying: "We have reached a tipping point. Inequality can no longer be treated as an afterthought. We need to focus the debate on how the benefits of growth are distributed. Our report *In it Together* and our work on inclusive growth have clearly shown that there doesn't have to be a trade-off between growth and equality. On the contrary, the opening up of opportunity can spur stronger economic performance and improve living standards across the board!" In his speech delivered at the Brookings Institute, OECD Secretary-General Gurría explains that OECD's numbers tell a clear-cut story of how our traditional economic growth agenda has neglected inclusiveness.

Table 2 demonstrates that the top 10 percent of United States controlled 75.4 percent of the nation's wealth in 2013, topping the nine major affluent nations in Europe.

---

74 The CBPP was founded in 1981 to analyze federal budget priorities, with particular emphasis on the impact of various budget choices on low-income Americans.

	Top 10% own (1)	Rank	Gini Index (2)
United States	**75.4**	1	0.378
Denmark	72.2	2	0.248
Switzerland	71.5	3	0.345
Sweden	71.1	4	0.259
Norway	65.9	5	0.25
Germany	61.7	6	0.295
Canada	57.4	7	0.32
United Kingdom	53.3	8	0.345
France	51.8	9	0.29
Finland	44.9	10	0.259

**Table 2: Wealth distribution: The United States
compared to advanced democratic nations**
Sources: (1) Credit Suisse Global Wealth Databank (2013).
(2) Gini Coefficient after taxes and transfers reported by OECD for later
2000s. The Gini Indices[75] consist of data available for 2008–15.

As of 2013, US wealth distribution to these 10 percenters had increased to 75.4 percent from 69.80 percent in 2007, according to Global Databank of Credit Suisse. William Domhoff, a research professor in psychology and sociology at the University of California, Santa Cruz, states however, "If we break the data down further and will find that 93 percent of all financial wealth is controlled by the top 10 percent of the country."[76] His controversial book *Who Rules America?* (published in the 1960s) eventually became American reality after a half century. The only industrialized nation with a higher concentration of wealth in the top 10 percent than the United States was Switzerland at 71.3 percent back in 2000. But in 2013, the United States became number one in the world, with the highest concentration of wealth in the top 10 percent. Also, the United States has the highest income inequality with the highest Gini coefficient (0.378) among these affluent countries.

---

75 Gini Index: The index is based on the Gini coefficient, a statistical dispersion measurement that ranks income distribution on a scale between 0 and 1, with 0 representing perfect equality and 1 worst inequality. The Gini coefficient summarizes income inequality in a single number and is one of the most commonly used measures of income inequality. The measure has been in use since its development by Italian statistician Corrado Gini in 1921.

76 Source: http://www2.ucsc.edu/whorulesamerica/power/wealth.html.

It's about time Congress acknowledges that the Republican supply-side economic policy has performed very poorly over the past thirty years. In fact, by weakening labor standards (including minimum wage, expanding globalization of labor import, erosion of the social-safety net, and the move toward fewer and weaker unions), Congress has created a wealth concentration at the top while the majority of Americans are sinking or struggling to stay afloat. Republican policies have served to erode the bargaining power of most workers, widen wage inequality, and deplete access to good jobs. In the past ten years, even workers with a college degree have failed to see any real wage growth. According to Sam Pizzigati, author of *Greed and Good,* the wealth disparity is the result of corporations squeezing more profits from workers.

SUPPLY-SIDE AND DEMAND-SIDE ECONOMICS

The bubble economies over the past thirty years helped corporate executives and rich owners of mega corporations pump up their income. In 1980, the average CEO made fifty times more money than the average worker, but today the average CEO makes almost three hundred times. Without a strong congressional action for change, this trend will undoubtedly continue. This strongly suggests that the Keynesian theory of "demand-side economics" is obviously much better option than supply-side economic theory in solving the problem of income inequality.[77] Keynes's view that governments should play a major role in economic management contrasts with the laissez-faire economics of Adam Smith, which held that economies function best when markets

---

77 Keynesian economics (demand-side economics): This is a school of macroeconomic thought based on the ideas of twentieth-century English economist John Maynard Keynes. This theory stands at the opposite side of supply-side economics. Keynesian economics argues that private-sector decisions sometimes lead to inefficient macroeconomic outcomes and, therefore, advocates active policy responses by the public sector, including monetary-policy actions by the central bank and fiscal-policy actions by the government to stabilize output over the business cycle. Demand-side economics is an economic theory that suggests that economic stimulation comes best from increasing the demand for goods and services. This concept is usually placed in direct opposition to supply-side economics. The idea is that, to stimulate growth, a government should lower taxes on the middle and working class, increase government spending, and increase taxes on the wealthy.

are left free of government intervention. Keynesian economics advocates a mixed economy (predominantly private sector, but with a significant role of government), and it served well as the economic model during the latter part of the Great Depression, World War II, and the postwar economic expansion (1945–73). The economic programs, mainly implementations of Keynesian economic policies, between 1933 and 1936 were passed by Congress during the first term of President Franklin D. Roosevelt during the Great Depression. Consequently, with the resulting new prosperity, consumer expenditures rose by nearly 50 percent, from $61.7 billion at the start of the war to $98.5 billion by 1944. Individual savings accounts climbed almost sevenfold during the course of the war. The share of total income held by the top 5 percent of wage earners fell from 22 percent to 17 percent, while the bottom 40 percent increased their share of the economic pie. In addition, during the course of the war the American population earning less than $3,000 (in 1968 dollars) fell by half, as stated by American historian William H. Chafe: "With full employment, higher wages and social-welfare benefits provided under government regulations, American workers experienced a level of well-being that, for many, had never occurred before."

To evaluate and analyze the economic well-being of citizens, economic efficiency, and the resulting income distribution associated with it—these are all part of congressional wisdom needed to bring about appropriate action plans to solve the inequality problem. In a nation of Christianity—which composes over 85 percent of Congress—with the highest records in inequality of income and wealth, the government needs more than just economic theory. This invokes the civic virtue of policy makers discussed in the previous chapter of this book. Each congressional member needs to ponder the effect of inequality and how it affects the nation's destiny.

I would not argue that the material abundance of those who have been working hard is God's blessing, but in the end the wealth is to be shared with brothers who are in need. Sadly, very few rich Americans are concerned about the humanistic morality of compassion, not to mention the prospects of true prosperity of the nation. The failure by those sitting on the mount of wealth to accept the moral obligation of sharing their wealth with the people who help them get rich by participating in the production of their goods and services clearly suggests that Christian morality has been thrown out of an American land that was once a God-loving nation. I hope good Christians agree that, on the grand scale of economics, the "supply side" is God's blessings and the "distribution side" is the government's duty to satisfy demand-side economics by redistributing the supply-side's blessings, remembering that in the circle of God's kingdom, all humans are equally bound and cherished by God's harmonic law (Φ) to thrive in peace and abundance.

Chapter 10

REALITY OF INEQUALITY

Income inequality itself may not be the cause of poverty; however, the very factors that create inequality cause poverty. Without going through details, I want to briefly summarize these factors in two major categories that I believe are triggering poverty: (1) excess freedom of capitalists (mega corporations with their owners and managers) and their control of labor market and (2) limitation of the social mobility of poor people. Thus, inequality and poverty grow in tandem fashion as shown by table 3 below.

	Gini Index [78]	Poverty Rate [79]
United States	**0.38**	**17.6**
Switzerland	0.35	9.4
United Kingdom	0.35	10.5
Canada	0.32	11.8
Germany	0.30	8.4
France	0.30	8.1
Sweeden	0.26	9.0
Finland	0.26	7.1
Norway	0.25	8.1
Denmark	0.25	5.4

Table3: Income inequality and poverty

78 OECD Report of Income Inequality for 2012–13.
79 OECD Income Distribution Database—Poverty (Data available for 2012–13).

The United States has the highest poverty rate among advanced nations, as shown in the table 3. The 2014 Census Bureau Poverty Rate Report shows that black Americans were hit the hardest at 26.2 percent; for Hispanics, the poverty rate was 23.6 percent; and for whites, 12.7 percent. These numbers translate that more than two people out of ten are in poverty in the United States, which is quite an unsettling reality. While the Census Bureau reported that the US median household income had reached almost $53,657 in 2014, those who are in poverty live on much less than a half of median income level. According to the US Census Bureau, the weighted average poverty-threshold amount for one person was $12,071 and for a family of four was $24,230 in 2014.

WHAT IS POVERTY?

The word "poverty" evokes strong emotions and many questions. In the United States, the official poverty thresholds are set by the Office of Management and Budget (OMB), defining persons with income less than that deemed sufficient to purchase basic needs—food, shelter, clothing, and other essentials. In simple terms, poverty is a chronic and debilitating condition that affects the mind, body, and soul of humankind. Young children are especially vulnerable to the negative effects of frequent change, disruption, and uncertainty. Developing children need reliable caregivers who offer high stability. Otherwise, their brains will typically develop adverse adaptive responses. Chronic socioeconomic deprivation can create environments that undermine the development of intelligence, the capacity for self-determination, and self-efficacy. Compared with their more affluent peers, low-income children form more stress-ridden attachments with parents or adult caregivers and have difficulty establishing friendships with children their own age. They are more likely to believe that their parents are uninterested in their activities, to receive less positive reinforcement from teachers, and to experience more turbulent or unhealthy friendships. Common issues in low-income families include depression, chemical dependence, and hectic work schedules—all factors that interfere with the healthy attachments that foster children's self-esteem, a sense of mastery of their environment, and optimistic attitudes. Poor children often feel isolated and unloved that kick off a downward spiral of unhappy life events, including poor academic performance, behavioral problems, dropping out of school, and drug abuse. These events tend to rule out college as an option and perpetuate the cycle of poverty. Children of immigrants make up more than 20 percent of the total child poverty cases in the United States. A massive influx of immigrants entering the United States every year competes for low-wage jobs. The statistical link between low-wage earners and increased childbearing suggests that young girls with the least financial independence are often most vulnerable to pregnancy as they are more likely to embrace motherhood in their current positions perceiving that socioeconomic success is not achievable to them. And their ensuing calamity is about a lack of basic necessities and a lack of security with unprotected children with them.

WHY IS THE US-POVERTY RATE THE HIGHEST AMONG ADVANCED NATIONS?

The United States was ranked the sixth worst among 173 countries on income equality[80] measured by the Gini index showing the highest poverty rate among the ten best known welfare states in the western world today as shown in table 3 of this chapter.

CBO reported that for the 1979–2007 period, after-tax income of households in the top 1 percent of earners grew by 275 percent, compared to 18 percent for the bottom fifth of households as shown in figure 9. Let's be reminded that not all these people in poverty are nonworking. The real median earnings of full-time, year-round working men and women declined by 2.2 percent in 2014 from 2007, the year before the most recent recession. And, for virtually the entire period of 1979–2012, wage growth for most workers has been stagnant. The median worker saw an increase of just 5.0 percent between 1979 and 2012, while the bottom

---

80 Credit Suisse Research Institute Global Wealth Databook 2013.

twentieth percentile worker saw wage erosion of 0.4 percent. In fact, ever since 1979, the vast majority of American workers have seen their hourly wages stagnate or decline. This is despite real GDP growth of 157 percent and net productivity growth of 74.5 percent over the same period. Such divergence indicates an overall shift of the national income shared by workers and how much is taken by owners of corporations. The income share going to workers decreased as their real-wage growth has not been in line with productivity growth. In short, the potential for broad-based wage growth has existed over the past three and a half decades, but these economic opportunities have largely bypassed the vast majority of workers. The poor performance of American workers' wages in recent decades, particularly their failure to grow at anywhere near the pace of overall productivity, is the United States's serious economic challenge in comparing with the prosperity period of 1947 until 1979 when the average hourly wage tracked steadily upward as productivity increased. During this period, the very rich took home a much smaller proportion of total national income, and the nation as a whole grew faster as workers' wages surged. During this period, the bottom–fifth's income growth was 118 percent, compared to 86 percent growth for the top fifth. But the trend lines from 1979 to 2007 are quite different, as shown in figure 9.

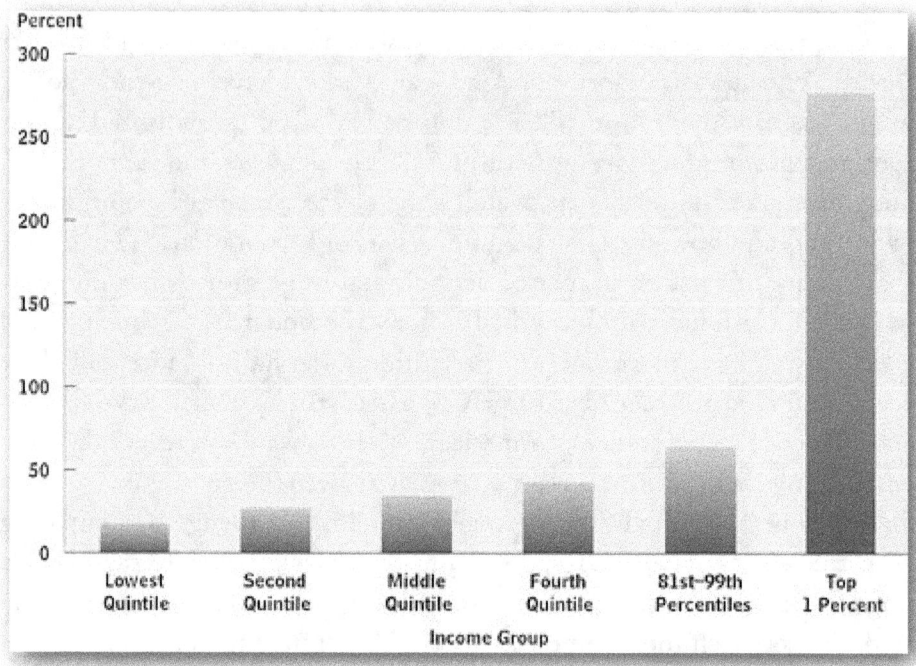

Figure 9: Growth in real after-tax income from 1979 to 2007[81]

For instance, the trend of income growth from 1979 to 2007 completely reversed, showing 74 percent growth (after tax) for the top 20 percent with a much smaller growth for the bottom 20 percent. A further income disparity between the top 1 percent and 99 percent poor is displayed as time went on. The average inflation-adjusted income of the bottom 99 percent of taxpayers grew by only 18.9 percent between 1979 and 2007. Over the same period, the average income of the top 1 percent of taxpayers grew by 275 percent. This lopsided income growth means that the top 1 percent of taxpayers captured 53.9 percent of all income growth over the period[82] increasing the gap further between the poor and the rich.

Note that the bottom 20 percent income has been stagnating or shrinking, and such statistical revelation is translated into the reality of American

---

81 Source: Congressional Budget Office, https://www.cbo.gov.
82 Source: Estelle Sommeiller and Mark Price, Economic Policy Institute Report (EPI), February 19, 2014.

poverty. You may have guessed that a given size of America's pie of wealth is encroached relentlessly year after year by those at the top, leaving the majority of people with small pieces and crumbs. In 2007, the top 20 percent of the wealthy possessed 80 percent of all financial assets in the United States. But shockingly as of 2010, the top 10 percent richest owned 85 percent of financial assets as shown in figure 10 below.

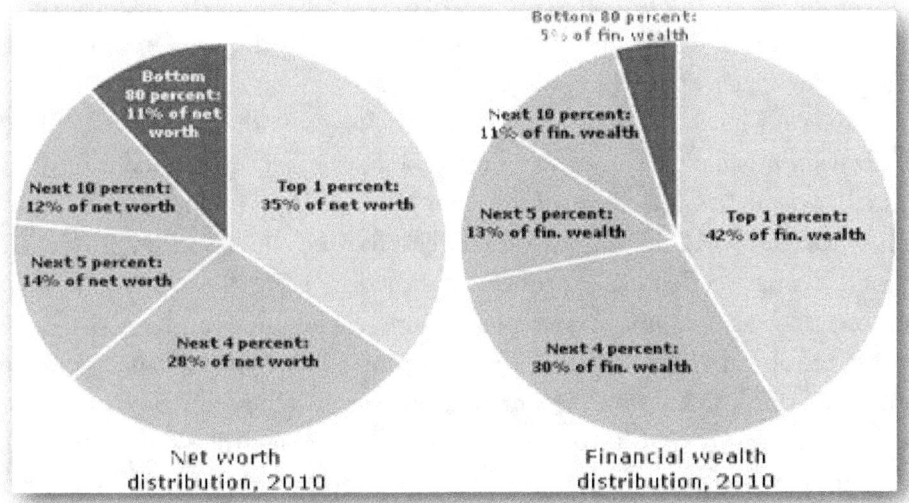

Net worth distribution, 2010

Financial wealth distribution, 2010

Figure 10: 2010 Wealth distribution by type of asset[83]

On the other end of the spectrum, the average real hourly earnings for all employees actually declined by 4 percent in real median hourly earnings between 2009 and 2014, according to salary data from the Bureau of Labor Statistics. While average wages fall and almost twenty million people remain unemployed, America's slow economic recovery has yet almost entirely benefited corporations and their executives. For example, the pay of Wisconsin's top corporate executives rose an average of 27 percent in 2010, a year when official unemployment hovered around 9 percent and pay to the average worker in the state fell. The stocks of these corporations went up by 28 percent on average, which highlights that executives' earnings were justified in light of

---

83 Source: William Domhoff, *"Who Rules America?"* http://www2.ucsc.edu/whorulesamerica/ power/wealth.html.

stock price increase.[84] On a national level, the executive compensation increase was much higher: real CEO compensation at big firms rose 36 percent, while average workers' salaries increased only 2.6 percent in 2010, according to the GMI Pay Survey.[85] Observing the reality of such inequality of income distribution, the OECD Secretary-General José Ángel Gurría warned of the dangers posed by inequality and the need for governments to tackle it: "Growing inequality is divisive. It polarizes societies, it divides regions within countries, and it carves up the world between rich and poor. Greater income inequality stifles upward mobility between generations, making it harder for talented and hardworking people to get the rewards they deserve. Ignoring increasing inequality is not an option. The largest part of the increase in inequality comes from changes in the labor markets. This is where governments must act."In a 2012 article, the OECD emphasized the reduction or elimination of tax breaks that primarily benefit those who are well off. Key policy recommendations for OECD countries include: "The growing share of income going to top earners means that this group now has a greater capacity to pay taxes. In this context governments may reexamine the redistributive role of taxation to ensure that wealthier individuals contribute their fair share of the tax burden. Governments must tackle record gap between rich and poor."[86]

No doubt the perilous income inequality and rising poverty should be the centerpiece of the US-congressional agenda. Nevertheless, so far Congress's main focus has been on budget cuts to programs designed to protect families from hardship, where the larger population feels the pain of continuing unemployment and the loss of what little wealth they have in their homes. The growing gap and heavy concentration of wealth in the top 20 percent of

---

84 Source: The Journal Sentinel, WI, May 14, 2011.

85 GMI Ratings, the leading independent provider of global corporate-governance and ESG ratings and research, is the combined entity of Governance Metrics International, The Corporate Library and Audit Integrity, which all merged in December 2010. GMI Ratings, covering more than sixty-four hundred companies worldwide, are built on extensive research and modeling that incorporate a broad spectrum of Environmental, Social and Governance (ESG) metrics. GMI Ratings is a signatory to the United Nations–backed Principles for Responsible Investment Initiative.

86 OECD, "Reducing Income Inequality while Boosting Economic Growth," January 23, 2012. See full synopsis of OECD in the bibliography of this book.

the US population challenge the capitalistic government policy that allows this differential to continue to expand. The challenge is especially serious as the broader population feels increasing pain from reduction in programs like Medicare, Medicaid, and food stamps—all designed and intended to help assuage some of the economic distress.

While some rich people pay $500,000 for a bottle of wine or $150 million for a painting, there are millions of homeless people roaming the streets begging for food in the United States. One approximation of the annual number of homeless people in America is from a study by the National Law Center on Homelessness and Poverty, which estimates that people experiencing homelessness were between 2.3 and 3.5 million in 2008 (although the US Department of Housing and Urban Development estimated only 671,888). In 2010, the federal government found that 1.6 million people had experienced homelessness at some point. While that figure is still cited, the National Coalition for the Homeless tried to compensate for undercounting and put the figure at approximately 3.5 million. The question of how many people are homeless is both misleading and nearly impossible to answer in any precise way, as seen by the varying estimates and methodologies. But poor people are at risk of homelessness—those in poverty, those living with friends and family, and those paying more than half their income for housing. Despite some progresses following the recession, challenges still remain. Although the overall economy has started to recover, this improvement does not appear to be penetrating lower-income populations. A steady decrease in federally subsidized housing, loose regulations on developers, and the foreclosure crisis have all helped jack up the nation's rate of homelessness. The lack of affordable housing cannot be overcome by the homeless-assistance system alone. Communities, states, and the federal government need to invest in affordable housing so that households are able to obtain and maintain housing independently in their own communities. Across the country, far too many men, women, and families with children experience homelessness. In the District of Columbia, in the shadow of our nation's capital, more than seven thousand people experience homelessness on any given night—sleeping outside, in a shelter, or in transitional housing. In the past five years, the city has seen a 12 percent increase in homelessness. It's not hard to guess that there are several million people out there looking for a roof over their heads and meals to survive. When it comes right down to it, the only difference between the homeless and those who have shelter is that the homeless do not have any family members who can support them. Government benefits have taken substantial cuts in recent years in spite of the fact that the recession has increased the number of homeless people who have lost a house to foreclosure or fallen too far behind on rent. The homeless assistance system, usually operated by a nonprofit agency or associated with a church, attempts to decrease homelessness by increasing the flow of people into permanent housing. But without a decrease in the number of people who become homeless, the homeless assistance system alone cannot deal with large population of homeless in their communities.

DOES THE US GOVERNMENT LIVE UP TO ITS MISSION STATEMENT?

When it comes to social and economic welfare, American citizens expect the government to assume the primary responsibility, trusting that the government is the body of their will. American citizens rely on the profound mission statement of the Constitution as their collective mission statement, agreeing to carry out the mission together with their government. The mission statement (The United States Constitution, Preamble) of the United States declares:

> We the people of the United States, in order to form a more perfect union, establish justice, insure domestic tranquility, provide for the common defense, promote the general welfare, and secure the blessings of liberty to ourselves and our posterity, do ordain and establish this Constitution for the United States of America.

The Constitution's preamble is the mission statement of the government— whose sole mission is none other than to serve the people, ensuring their happiness. But the role of Congress, especially in the past thirty-two years, has been estranged from this sacred mission statement. I want to point out several important words contained in the preamble: *people, perfect union, justice, domestic tranquility, and common defense.*

"We, the people" means all citizens of our nation, who jointly determine the nation's destiny through the common good—that is, creating social conditions that benefit all people. The Constitution is established and ordained by the people. The government derives its power and authority from the people, not the other way around. However, today's reality undoubtedly suggests that the majority of citizens' desires and voices—aimed at sustaining the principles of common good to secure equal prosperity for everyone—are not respected. In today's reality, *people* seems to mean the top 1 percent rich. Our government pays close attention to this minor group of powerful voices, not the other 99 percent of Americans who are the co-owners of the nation. What this means is, political access is concentrated at the top with an influential class that doesn't respond to the needs of poor people. The national policy-making process has been heavily influenced by the top 1 percent who, in seeking their self-interest more than the common good, control the rest of Americans by hiring and firing at their disposal. Trickling down benefits from the top 1 percent to the rest of the citizens stops at approximately the next 10 percent of citizens, who are inevitably loyal to their benefactors' interest. This leaves the majority of the population excluded from the influencing power to lead the nation's destiny.

A *perfect union* doesn't exist when the majority of citizens are struggling with poverty while the richest build their wall high against the poor. America is divided into two camps—the small but powerful rich and the large but powerless poor—making the latter a class of beggary citizens who are not as important as the former. Once proud middle-class Americans are now poor, having been eroded and gradually pushed into the poor camp over the past thirty years since the "trickle-down" economic policy began.

Peace is a state of harmony characterized by the absence of violent conflict and discordance. Peace represents prosperity in matters of social or economic welfare, the establishment of equality, and a working political order that serves the true interests of all. A *perfect union* is shattered when the government (Congress) neglects to exercise necessary civic virtues, siding only with the rich. Each of Congress's members must remember who sent them there, who they represent, and what the role of government is. The purpose and mission of the Congress is to serve its people as a steward, and none other. A perfect union can be restored when the nation reclaims Christian humanism, reviving the spirit of compassion embedded deeply in Christianity. Compassion is a heavenly melody that has to be shared with every soul to sustain the harmony. Compassion is the spirit of love commanded by God's harmonic law, which must be practiced by Congress with an appropriate civic virtue in a graceful way. What does love (compassion) look like? According to Saint Augustine of Hippo:

> It has the hands of helping others. It has the feet to hasten to the poor and needy. It has eyes to see misery and want. It has the ears to hear the sighs and sorrows of men. That is what Love looks like.

The underlying virtue of stewardship is this caring spirit. The core of harmonic law is the spirit of love. Congress members must remember that the nation's *perfect union* can be formed only by embracing everyone in it by equitable distribution of national income/wealth, not letting the rich minority control the nation's destiny. A *perfect union* represents the perfect health of a nation—similar to the perfect circulation of blood and energy in the body for physical health. A healthy society depends on the smooth flow of communication between the government and its people in obedience to God's harmonic law.

American citizens have been watching Congress divided between conservative Republicans and liberal Democrats, creating a hard gridlock—competing and wrestling, instead of agreeing on the common good for the people. As far as citizens are concerned, they have one Congress entrusted with the mission for the common good. The doctrine of human *justice* doesn't work as long as the gap between the rich and poor keeps expanding. When the richest oligarchy hoards the majority of the nation's wealth for its greedy interest leaving the majority of that nation's voices muffled in dark poverty, human justice disappears into the cracks created by poor stewardship of government. Let's remember that America is built on faith in God, not on greed. Thus, we are reminded of Saint Augustine's profound statement: "Find out how much God has given you and from it take what you need; the remainder is needed by others."

Domestic tranquility doesn't exist when the majority of citizens struggle to make ends meet in the shadow of poverty. The definition of poverty fundamentally is a denial of choices and opportunities and a violation of human dignity. This means a lack of basic capacity to participate effectively in society. It means not having enough to feed and clothe a family, not having a job to earn one's living, not having access to credit. It means insecurity, powerlessness, and exclusion of individuals, households, and communities. It means susceptibility to violence, and it often implies living in marginal or fragile environments. In short, poverty means the inability to acquire the basic goods and services necessary for survival with dignity.

Poverty also encompasses low levels of health and education, poor access to clean water and sanitation, inadequate physical security, lack of voice, and insufficient capacity and opportunity to better one's life. Poverty is a living hell, strapping the poor into an inescapably deep pit. Poverty breeds and spreads evil forces: violence, crime, bodily diseases, mental distress, social cynicism, apathy, fear, anger, and terrorism against the nation, demoralizing the nation's spirit. The eradication of poverty is thus the first step toward domestic tranquility and is *common defense* to protect the state of happiness of all citizens.

Chapter 11

CONSEQUENCES OF INEQUALITY

The United States ranks the highest in income and wealth inequality among advanced nations as shown in table 2 (chapter 9). A recent report by the Equality Trust (an independent campaign group working to reduce income inequality in the United Kingdom) outlined numerous social maladies caused by income inequality. I want to highlight those categories of inequality-caused maladies here to emphasize the imperativeness of government action.

PHYSICAL HEALTH AND LIFE EXPECTANCY

There are an overwhelming number of worldwide research studies addressing income inequality in relation to various aspects of human health. Evidences provided by these reports indicate that the extent of socioeconomic disparities—the size of the gap in income and wealth between the top and bottom of society—is an important determinant of the health achievement of society, independent of the average standard of living indicated by GDP per capita income. In other words, the health of a population depends not on the size of the economic pie (generally stated as GDP) but on how the pie is shared. Wealthy countries with more equitable income distributions, such as Sweden and Japan, have higher life expectancies than does the United States, despite their lower GDP. Likewise, countries, such as Costa Rica, with low GDP but remarkably high life expectancy, tend to have more equitable distribution of income.

Furthermore, a recent study across US metropolitan areas found that areas with high income inequality had an excess of fatalities compared to areas with low inequality. A 2009 study reported in the *British Medical Journal* attempted to quantify the number of deaths that could be attributed to economic inequality among the thirty rich countries that make up the OECD. The study concluded that almost 884,000 excess deaths per year in the United States could be attributed to the high level of income inequality.

Life expectancy, infant mortality, low birth weight, and self-rated health have repeatedly been shown to be worse in more unequal societies. The United States was the highest in mortality rate among nineteen advanced nations during the periods 1997–98 and 2002–3.[87] Also, in a twenty-year analysis of newborn death rates around the world, ranking from the lowest to highest the United States ranked forty-first out of forty-five among industrialized countries.[88]

The most consistent interpretation of all the evidences is that inequality makes life extremely stressful. Chronic stress is one of the main causes of many diseases, such as cardiovascular disease, diseases of the immune system, and a host of others including mental disorders.

MENTAL HEALTH

Approximately 20 percent of American adults experience some sort of mental illness and 5 percent suffer from a severe case, according to the 2010 National Survey on Drug Use and Health conducted by Mental Health America (formerly known as the National Mental Health Association, a leading nonprofit organization helping people live mentally healthier lives). Another 2011 survey by the Centers for Disease Control and Prevention (CDC) states that

---

87 Based on a research supported by the Commonwealth Fund and published in the January 2008 issue of *Health Affairs*.

88 Source: CNN report on Women's Health, August 31, 2011.

during 2007–8, an estimated 47.8 million ambulatory care visits were made by patients with primary mental-health diagnoses, which constituted approximately 5 percent of all ambulatory-care visits made in the United States during those two years. Women made 29.4 million of the visits, compared with 18.5 million for men. Of all mental illness and related visits, the greatest proportion of visits (31 percent) was made by patients with depressive disorder, followed by 23 percent of visits among those with schizophrenia and other psychotic disorders.

Another survey conducted by the same organization in 2004 reported that 25 percent of adults in the United States had a mental illness in 2003. The statistics of ten years (2004–14) have not improved, showing that every year about 42.5 millions of American adults (or 18.2 percent of the total adult population in the United States) suffers from mental illness, including conditions such as depression, bipolar disorder, and schizophrenia. The Equality Trust generated a chart (figure 11) showing the relationship between mental illness and income inequality among thirteen developed countries, which highlights the United States as the highest among these advanced nations.

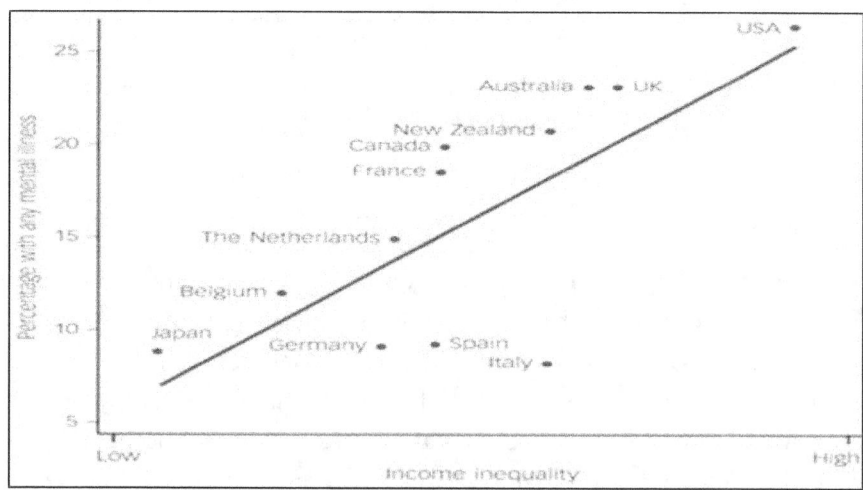

Figure 11: Mental illness and inequality[89]

---

89 Source: Equality Trust. https://www.equalitytrust.org.uk /mental-health.

Mental illness undoubtedly is much more common in countries with more economic inequality. Simply put, people in more equal societies are far less likely to experience mental illness. A 2009 article on mental illness and inequality published by the World Health Organization (WHO) stressed that inequality has the most profound and far-reaching consequences for individuals and the wider society. The study, which draws on research from throughout Europe, concluded that mental-health difficulties are most pronounced in countries that have high levels of income and social inequality. The report's author, Lynne Friedli, warns that governments need to sit up and take notice, and that policy makers need to face up to the fact that marked improvements in mental health and well-being will depend on first tackling the gap between the rich and poor. The report stressed: "There is overwhelming evidence that inequality is a key cause of stress coping with material deprivation."

In general, the adverse impact of stress is greater in societies where more inequality exists and where people feel worse off than others. Simply put, inequality makes social relations stressful by increasing status differences and competition. Such compelling evidence should urge the US government (Congress) to address the issue of economic inequality directly to mend comprehensive national health rather than narrowly focusing on medical services.

DRUG ABUSE AND VIOLENCE

Other problems besides health issues are seriously pronounced in highly unequal society, including drug abuse, imprisonment, obesity, violence, and teen pregnancy. The following chart (figure 12) demonstrates that the United States far exceeds any other advanced countries in these problems.

Figure 12: Drug abuse, violence, imprisonment, obesity, and teenage births[90]

Many Americans believe that drug abuse is not their problem. They have a misconception that drug users belong to a certain segment of society different from their own or that drug abuse is remote from their environment. They are wrong. Almost three-quarters of drug users are employed or engaged in some kind of productive work. Drug use and drug-related crime are among our nation's most pressing social problems. Approximately 45 percent of Americans know someone with a substance abuse problem. Illegal drug use costed the nation more than $193 billion in 2007, according to a study released on May 26, 2011, by the US Justice Department's National Drug Intelligence Center. The National Institute on Drug Abuse (NIDA) stated in a 2014 report that the combination of abuse of tobacco, alcohol, and illicit

---

90 Source: Richard Wilkinson and Kate Pickett, *The Spirit Level* (London: Allen Lane, 2009).

drugs costs the nation more than $700 billion annually, relating to crime, lost work productivity, and health care.

Besides drug abuse, violence is another prevalent problem in unequal societies. One can label most violence as drug-related, mental-disorder-related or poverty-related crimes. Whatever the direct influence behind the violence may be, it stems from the various conflicts and discontent spread by inequality in society. According to a research conducted by Professor Richard Wilkinson of the University of Nottingham, very unequal societies tend to have higher crime rates than those societies that are economically challenged but have more equality. Congressman Mike Honda has indicated that the United States wastes approximately $361 billion per year on cost related to violent crime, homicides, incarceration, and policing availability of small arms. (Mike Honda, a Democrat representing California, serves on the House Budget and Appropriations committees.)

PRISON-POPULATION GROWTH

The US-imprisonment rate is fourteen times the rate of Japan, and between the states there are even big differences, where Louisiana imprisons people at a rate six times higher than Minnesota. According to a research paper by the Institute for Research on Poverty[91], from 1995 to 2000, incarceration increased steeply as the violent-crime rate plummeted. These simple aggregate trends lend at least to the idea that inequality, not crime, is behind the prison boom. Figure 13 below, produced by Justice Policy Institute,[92] proves that imprisonment is undoubtedly related to inequality and shows that the prison boom actually started with the "trickle-down" economic policy in the 1980s.

---

91 Article: *Crime, Punishment, and American Inequality by* Institute for Research on Poverty, University of Wisconsin–Madison 32, no. 2 (Fall/Winter 2015–16).

92 As a national nonprofit organization, JPI is dedicated to reducing the use of incarceration and the justice system by promoting fair and effective policies.

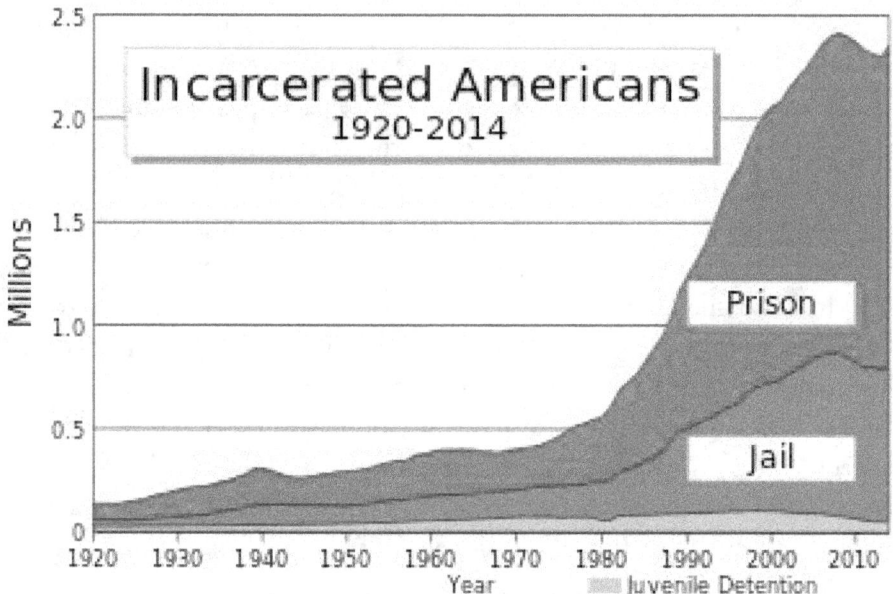

Figure 13: Inequality and prison[93]

The United States has the highest rate of incarceration in the world according to the National Council on Crime and Delinquency report issued in January 2010. We can discuss this in more detail. In 2008 there were 1,609,759 inmates, which increased to 2,220,300 in 2013. Additionally, 4,751,400 adults in 2013 were on probation or on parole. Thus in total, 6,899,000 adults were under correctional supervision in 2013.[94] The US rate of incarceration, with nearly 1 out of every 100 adults in prison or jail, is five to ten times higher than the rates in Western Europe and other democratic nations. The United States has about 5 percent of the world's population, but has 25 percent of the world's prisoners with the staggering cost of $63.4 billion a year. This translates into $31,307 per year per inmate.

The increase of incarceration slowly began in the early 1970s as the political response to increased drug use and urban violence. Then prison

---

93 Source: Justice Policy Institute Report, Washington, DC, http://www.justicepolicy.org/.

94 Source: US Bureau of Justice Statistics (BJS).

population exploded with a 700 percent increase in three decades (1977–2008) as one can visualize from figure 13. It should be noted that only 52 percent of sentenced prisoners in state prisons during 2008 were in for violent crimes according to Bureau of Justice Statistics, meaning that almost half of the inmates were taken in for nonviolent crimes. The US-prison population is largely drawn from the most disadvantaged part of the nation's population: mostly men under age forty, disproportionately in minority, and poor.

OBESITY AND TEEN PREGNANCY

Although it does not fall into the category of a punishable crime, another widespread problem in unequal societies is the obesity of the population. Obesity is increasing rapidly throughout the developed world, with rates doubling in some countries in just a few years. In the United States, three-quarters of the population is overweight and close to one-third is obese. Obesity increases the risk of hypertension, late-onset diabetes, cardiovascular disease, gallbladder disease, and some cancers. The trends in children's obesity are likely to lead to shorter life expectancies for today's youth, which would be the first reversal in life expectancy since the nineteenth century. Similarly, these children are likely to do less well at school, are more likely to use drugs, and are more likely to become teenage parents.

Teenage-motherhood rates rise in societies with more inequality. The differences in teen-birth rates between countries are striking. In the United States, the teenage-birth rate is fifty-two per one thousand women aged fifteen to nineteen, more than ten times higher than Japan. Babies born to teenage mothers are more likely to have low birth weight, to be born prematurely, and to be at higher risk of dying in infancy. (The high US infant-death rate mentioned in the previous physical-health section is predominantly related to teenage births.) As they grow up, these children are at greater risk of educational failure, juvenile crime, and becoming teenage parents themselves. Girls who give birth as teenagers are more likely to be poor and uneducated. Teenage motherhood is part of the intergenerational cycle of deprivation and social exclusion, according to the *American Journal of Public Health*. Various other researchers have reached the same conclusion on inequality in the United States.

LOW GLOBAL PEACE INDEX

The summation of problems in health, drug abuse, violence, imprisonment, obesity, and teenage birth is reflected in the Global Peace Index developed by the Institute for Economics and Peace.[95] The Index summarizes the degree of peacefulness a nation sustains. The 2014 GPI shows that the United States ranks 101st, while neighboring Canada (the second largest country in world) is the seventh among 153 countries worldwide. Based on the actual scores extracted from the IEP's Global Peace Index, I generated the following chart (figure 14) to display the relative rankings of ten countries for comparison purposes. Nine of those countries fare far better than the United States in real scores. For instance, Germany is the seventeenth (1.423) and Denmark is the second in GPI ranks (1.193), while the United States is the 101st among 153 countries with a score of 2.137. In fact, US peacefulness is more on par with those economically struggling countries such as Algeria, the Dominican Republic, Uganda, and other underdeveloped nations. To put it differently, all the advanced nations are far ahead of the United States in acceptable peacefulness. Figure 14 is based on data extracted from GPI 2014; the order of rank begins with the most peaceful nation to least peaceful one on the right.

---

95 **Global Peace Index (GPI):** Twenty-three indicators of the existence or absence of peace were chosen in order to rank the nations in GPI, which can be divided into three broad categories: ongoing, domestic, and international conflict; safety and security in society; and militarization. The GPI is the world's leading measure of national peacefulness developed by the Institute for Economics and Peace (IEP), a nonprofit research organization dedicated to shifting the world's focus to peace as a positive, achievable, and tangible measure of human well-being and progress. Now in its fifth year, it ranks 153 nations according to their "absence of violence." It seeks to identify the components of a peaceful society and to rank the countries of the world by their "peacefulness." Countries are scored on a range from 1 to 5, where 1 = most peaceful. The United States has the highest score, which means it's the worst in its degree of peacefulness.

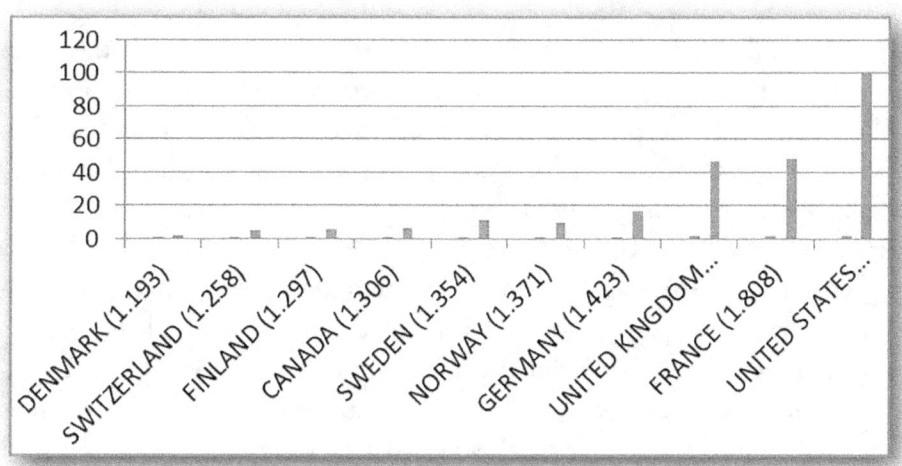

Figure 14: Peace rankings of advanced nations
(Source: Author's analysis based on GPI 2014.)

The United States is the richest nation in the world in terms of GDP; however, its national peacefulness is at the level of underdeveloped nations, drifting behind all other advanced nations. This means American civilization is heading backward. During three centuries of our nation's history, the American people and government have believed that the best way of improving the quality of life of people and national prosperity was to raise material living standards via economic growth. The government therefore has aggressively pursued national economic growth, or GDP growth. But we have come to realize that economic growth that depends heavily on a small number of wealthy people is not a real growth of economy or national prosperity. The real growth is collective prosperity, where all citizens are equally doing well.

Measures of well-being and peacefulness of the nation are not dependent on economic growth dominated by the minority rich. This type of growth, in fact, is similar to feudalism. With such selective growth, not only has economic growth ceased to bring social benefits to citizens, but it now threatens the nation's domestic peace, with mounting social problems. On the one hand, when the country gets richer by protecting the rich minority and ignoring the welfare of the rest of its citizens, it creates many social problems, shattering the unity of the nation and thus increasing perils to peace. On the other hand, countries with smaller income differences between rich and poor are more cohesive, united, and peaceful, wherein community life is stronger, levels of trust are higher, and of course, there is much less violence. In other words, when the vast majority of the population benefits from greater equality, the nation is united and more peaceful.

Therefore, if societies have to choose between greater equality and economic growth, people who have wisdom in rich countries clearly reach a point that equality is the rational choice. A more equal society provides an environment in which business can operate more efficiently. There are many empirical studies suggesting that more equal societies have better economic performance, as demonstrated by the Nordic countries. Those rich countries with more income equality tend to spend a higher proportion of their gross national income on the welfare of their people, such as medical, education, old-age benefits, and comparably less on militarism, thus performing better on the Global Peace Index.

Is there a correlation between national peace and global peace? The answer is definitely yes. What people learn about human relations in their own society establishes their basic humanistic morality, which they then apply to the world at large. Remember that the quality of human relationships is better in more equal societies—they have lower levels of violence, higher levels of trust, and community life is stronger. These are the opposite of the divisive effects of inequality. In an unequal society with a powerful marker of status differentiation, inequality tells people that they are in a society with divergent interests, where they have to compete with one another and fend for themselves. In a society with high inequality, the stresses from poverty and low social status affect the nature of family life. This, in turn, affects children's emotional and cognitive development, ushering them into lives involving more conflict and self-reliance. In contrast, greater equality implies a degree of common interest and mutual interdependence, making people more empathetic and better at cooperation, sharing, and reciprocity.

POOR SOCIAL RELATIONS

Evidence on inequality in relation to trust and community life is telling us the same story (quite loudly). The quality of social relations is worse in societies with inequality. The researchers have shown repeatedly that high levels of trust are linked to low levels of inequality, both internationally and among the fifty US states. Inequality divides people by increasing social distances between the poor and rich, and widening differences in living standards and lifestyles. By increasing the gap between the rich and poor, the inequality renders the American dream far more likely to remain a dream for these poor people lacking social mobility and who are socially disconnected. It goes without saying that social cohesion, trust, and involvement in community life are an important part of the quality of life in any society. At the individual level, people who believe that most other people in their society in general can be trusted are also more inclined to have a positive view of their democratic institutions, to participate more in politics, and to be more active in civic organizations. In reality, most Americans sadly have a highly negative view of their government. In a cohesive society, people also give more to charity, and they are more tolerant toward one another. Trusting people also have a more optimistic view of their ability to have an influence over their own life and are happier with how their life is going.

People trust one another most in the Scandinavian countries among modernized nations worldwide. According to Bo Rothstein, an internationally acclaimed Swedish political scientist, "Government policies have a large impact on economic equality. Universal social programs that cater to the whole (or very broad sections) of society, such as we find in the Scandinavian countries, promote a more equitable distribution of wealth and more equality of opportunity in areas such as education and the labor market. Both types of equality lead to a greater sense of social solidarity—which spurs generalized trust."[96]

Without question, the government is the steward leading the direction toward social solidarity. Simply put, a government's fundamental duty is to foster peace for all. The peace I am referring to is an active peace—a state in

---

96 Bo Rothstein and Eric M. Uslaner, "All for All: Equality, Corruption and Social Trust," *World Politics* 58, no. 1 (October 2005): 41–72, (Cambridge University Press).

which the collective human conscience is actively aligned with the harmonic law of the universe. Thus, the government is serving the citizens in obedience of universal law to safeguard them against social maladies. Active peace demands actions by the government to resolve the underlying causes of human dysfunctions, such as mental disorder, violence, drug abuse, and other unhealthy human activities that destroy the peace of society.

Harmonic law can be practiced through appropriate and fair redistribution of a nation's wealth to close the gap between the wealthy and poor and bolster equality of opportunity for all so that everyone can have a fair chance to contribute to human society. Civilization can bloom much better in a peaceful environment, wherein the society values gentleness, brotherhood, and interdependence more than self-interest and self-reliance as social mores. History tells us that civilization is undeniably linked to the peace of the human mind in spiritual alignment with divine law—harmony (Φ)—and its application to our earthly societies. Under Christian humanism, active peace means propagation of goodwill and sharing burdens and blessings together. The wisdom of God no doubt imparts this idea to human intellect. Whether people adhere to religious principles or not, let's not forget that peace is the ultimate longing for all human beings, which is an indispensable part of human happiness. This calls for appropriate government policies by which everyone benefits, with no separation of winners and losers.

Chapter 12

EXCESSIVE MILITARY SPENDING

The US government in fiscal year 2015 appropriated $628 billion, over 54 percent of all federal discretionary spending of $1,160 billion, for military programs. Not surprisingly the US-military expenditure is more than 35 percent of entire world's military spending and dwarfs the next four largest military powers as shown in figure 15.

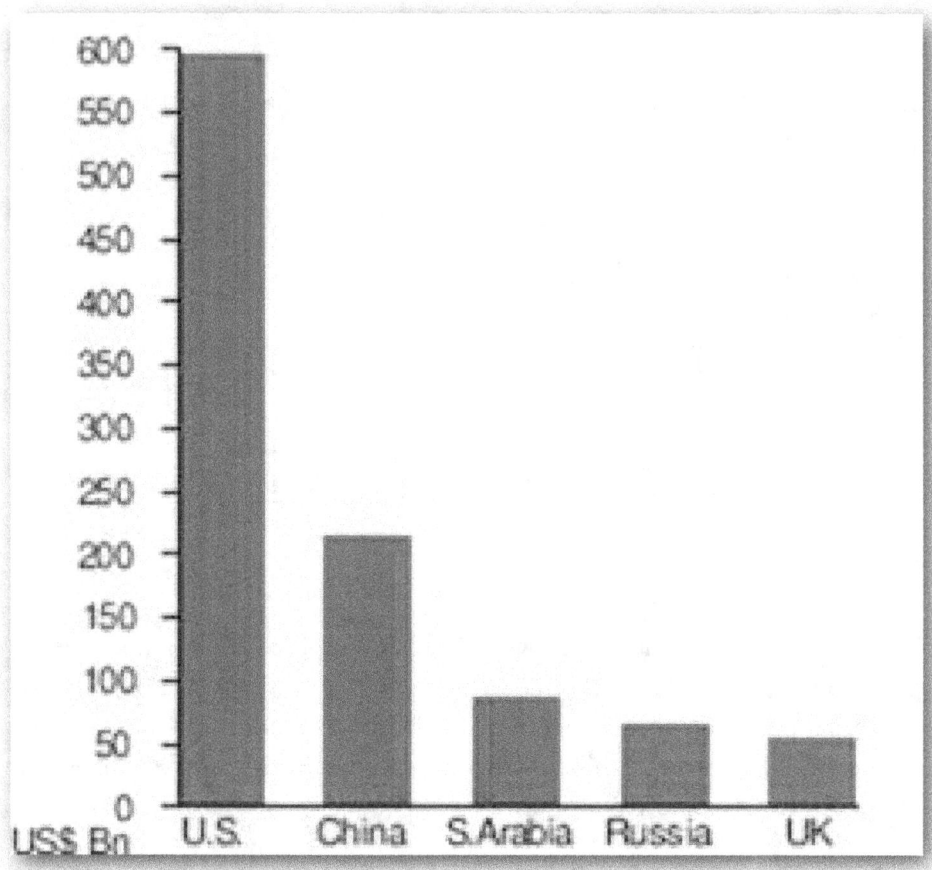

Figure 15: World's top five military spenders in 2015[97]

It's obvious that the US-taxpaying citizens did not vote for military spending to be so high, but the government allocated citizens' tax money into a towering military budget. Out of a total revenue of $3,250 billion in 2015, the government spent more than 18 percent for defense expenditure while incurring a $396.5 billion annual deficit.[98] To look at it another way, US military spending makes up 3.4 percent of its GDP. Note that the United States is the

97 Source: Stockholm International Peace Research Institute, "Trends in World Military Expenditure, 2015," April 2016.
98 Source: Office of Management and Budget (OMB), White House.

highest military spender in the world followed by China and Saudi Arabia in military expenditures.

WHO IS BENEFITING FROM BIG MILITARY SPENDING?

There is no plausible justification for spending a big chunk of national revenue in military expenditure, which does not add any tangible benefits to national prosperity although the defense industry routinely insists on its contribution to economic growth and added employment. It is not surprising to see that among the top one hundred arms-service companies in the world, the United States continues to account for the majority of arms sales in 2014, with thirty-eight companies, and seven of which are ranked in the top ten. These US companies' revenues represent 54.4 percent of the top one hundred total arms sales in the world in 2014.[99] In October 2011, the aerospace industry put out a report threatening that chopping the defense budget would put over a million Americans out of work. The reality, however, confirms that the large defense spending only benefits those large corporations and their shareholders and CEOs. For example, Lockheed's net earnings for 2010 were over $2.6 billion, and CEO Robert Stevens was paid $19.1 million in the same year. And Boeing's 2010 net income was $3.31 billion compared to $1.31 billion in 2009, increasing 152 percent. Boeing paid its CEO, Jim McNerney, $19.7 million in compensation. He boasted at the year-end 2011 earnings conference call (while the national unemployment rate was hovering around 9 percent), saying:

> Cash generation was exceptional with $1.1 billion in cash from operations in the quarter after making accelerated pension contributions of $1 billion and over $4.2 billion for the year, surpassing the prior year by more than $450 million. We paid $325 million in dividends in the quarter and $1.1 billion for the year as we continue to execute our $4 a share annual dividend payout. Share repurchases continued in the quarter and totaled almost 32 million shares for the year, enabling

---

99 Source: SIPRI, SIPRI Fact Sheet, December 2015.

the retirement of 7% of the outstanding shares. With this focus, we generated a 21% total shareholder return with 16% stock price appreciation and a 5% dividend yield.

Corporate CEOs, shareholders, and top-level employees of defense industries are the only ones who benefit from the high defense spending of our government. It is doubtful, on the one hand, if the wealth of these beneficiaries added any significant amount to national revenue, considering how low of an income tax they are paying. On the other hand, if the same amount of money spent on defense expenditures was distributed to welfare programs assisting the poor people, they would have likely spent all of it, rather than saving it, thus promoting economic growth by spurring consumer industries. The increase of consumption by these poor people would raise GDP by the same amount they spent, other things being equal. Since usually the United States separately taxes consumption by sales tax, an increase of consumption would also boost this type of state revenue, as well as import-duties revenue in the case of imported goods. Thus, decreasing defense expenditure and transferring the same money to the poor would allow considerable redistribution of wealth where needed.

MILITARY DOMINANCE DOES NOT ADD HAPPINESS TO CITIZENS

All in all, big spending on defense does not add national wealth nor provide welfare to the nation's citizens. This does not mean that a nation shouldn't spend any amount on defense at all. A moderate defense budget can be allocated to it—as low as 1 percent of GDP—which would be comparable to the defense spending of all other advanced nations. According to a 1985 empirical study conducted by P. C. Frederiksen and R. E. Looney, associate professors of economics at the Naval Postgraduate School in Monterey, California: "A model based on resource constraints predicts that defense can and does play an important role in the growth process of many developing countries, but for the rest of countries, the evidence would suggest a neutral role."

The citizens of the world are absolutely against military aggressions and high military budgets. The United Nations charter calls for the establishment of international peace and security through diversion of the world's human and economic resources away from armaments. That is to say the transferring of a large portion of military expenditure to social expenditure would highlight the virtuous quality of government (the next chapter of this book discusses more in detail.) It is quite obvious that military supremacy may deliver geopolitical dominance for power of intimidation, but it does not deliver economic prosperity and peace to the nation and the world.

Chapter 13

COLLECTIVE WISDOM FOR HUMAN HAPPINESS

A ristotle sets forth the importance of the political community as the source and sustainer of the happiness of human life. He emphasizes the necessity of human community because people depend on the community, not only for material necessities but also for education and moral habituation. Thus, community is formed by common action for the sake of the good life of all citizens. If a community is constituted by common action, then that community must aim at common good. And the community that does so in the highest degree, aiming at the most common good, embraces all citizens to promote those citizens' happiness. This should be the goal of all socioeconomic policies promulgated by government, whether founded on principles of republic democracy or social democracy. The best community is the one that is ruled by the best men—this idea has to be understood in terms of civic virtue.

PRINCIPLES OF CIVIC VIRTUE START WITH UNIVERSAL WISDOM OF HUMANISM AND COMPASSION

As discussed earlier, civic virtue refers to a firm and stable orientation of the political will directing all acts of government toward the common good of the society. Therefore, I cannot place too much emphasis on the importance of civic virtue for policy makers, since the citizens' happiness ultimately depends on the actions of those politicians and their intellectual reasoning. In terms of thought, we humans operate our physiological and intellectual thinking simultaneously and synergistically. It is, however, in the realm of intellectual thinking that we solve human problems and make improvements in our society. It is through rational improvement with God's wisdom that we increase our abilities of intellectual thinking to develop our virtue for ultimate happiness. The realm of intellectual thinking involves the capacities and skills we use in abstracting concepts, developing understanding, making judgments, affirming or denying propositions, reasoning and deducing conclusions, sharpening analytical skills, setting priorities, verifying deductions, and acquiring knowledge.

In most contexts, the terms "intellectual," "rational," and "problem solving" are interchangeable. As defined, the term "intellectual" is more generic than the term "rational," and "rational" is more generic than "problem solving." Thus, "intellectual" is an umbrella term that covers all abstract thinking, including rational thinking and problem solving. Rational thinking is more specific and refers to an aspect of intellectual thinking that in some manner involves reason. Problem solving is even more specific and refers to reasoning used in solving problems.

However, not all intellectual thinking involves reasoning, and not all reasoning is directed toward solving problems. Intellectual talents include our abilities to understand abstract concepts, to comprehend the difference between true and false, to distinguish valid from invalid reasoning, to choose priorities, and to intentionally apply decisions to activities. The application of our intellectual talents to matters at hand always involves reasoning and is therefore rational. Rational thinking in turn always in some manner employs reasoning. We can cure rational difficulties with intellectual means, such as refining definitions, double-checking facts, avoiding overgeneralizations, testing the validity of our deductions, expanding knowledge, learning to avoid logical fallacies, and so on. The intellectually sound person never forgets that perhaps he or she is wrong and the other person is right. Sound rational thinking, as it's defined, is intellectual activity in which we adequately use reason to solve problems in an unprejudiced manner. However, it should be mentioned that in the normal course of human affairs, the base of rational thinking is not necessarily associated with human virtue. The virtue is the humane element nurtured by the wisdom of God. The more policy makers learn to appreciate the requirements of civic virtue as a foundation of sound rational thinking, the more society can improve its collective happiness.

COLLECTIVE HUMAN VIRTUE AND OECD

Collective intellectual thinking, pooling individual virtue and rationalities together, can build a virtuous society that's sustainable for human happiness. Such collective intellectual thinking was born in our modern era. This group is called the OECD and was officially launched on September 30, 1961, but its roots go back to the rubble of Europe after World War II. Determined to avoid the mistakes of their predecessors in the wake of the world war, European leaders realized that the best way to ensure lasting peace was to encourage cooperation and reconstruction, rather than punish the defeated. Thus, the Organisation for European Economic Co-operation (OEEC) came into being on April 16, 1948, emerging from the Marshall Plan and the Conference of Sixteen, which sought to establish a permanent organization to continue work on a joint-recovery program and in particular to supervise the distribution of aid.

In September 1961, the OEEC was superseded by the worldwide body, OECD, which included the European founder countries of the OEEC, plus the United States and Canada. Its list of member countries has expanded over the years, with thirty-five countries today. They include many of the world's most advanced countries but also emerging countries like Mexico, Chile, and Turkey. The organization also works closely with emerging giants like China, India, and Brazil, and developing economies in Africa, Asia, Latin America, and the Caribbean. Its goal continues to be to build a stronger, cleaner, fairer world on planet Earth.

OECD uses its wealth of information on a broad range of topics to help every government foster prosperity and fight poverty through economic prosperity and fiscal stability. Its publications are the primary vehicle for the organization's intellectual output. OECD publishes periodic outlooks, annual overviews, and comparative statistics. Among them, the *OECD Economic Outlook* assesses prospects for every member and major nonmember economies. The *OECD Fact Book* is a key reference tool for everyone working on economic and policy issues. OECD's diligent economic surveys provide analyses and policy recommendations, and its Social Expenditure Database (SOCX) has been a very powerful data source. The SOCX was developed in order to serve a growing need for indicators of social policies, and it includes reliable and internationally comparable statistics on public and private social expenditure at various program levels. It provides a unique tool for monitoring trends in aggregate social expenditure and analyzing changes in its composition. In more specific terms, the underscored main social policy areas include: old age, survivors, incapacity-related benefits, health, family, active labor-market programs, unemployment, housing, and other related social-policy areas.

In a nutshell, OECD aims to promote policies that will improve the economic and social well-being of common people around the world. Thus, the organization keenly observes issues that directly affect the lives of ordinary people, such as how much they pay in taxes, how different countries' school systems are working to nurture their young people for their future, how different countries' pension systems provide for citizens in old age, how countries' public spending is allocated, and so on. Therefore, OECD-member countries worldwide regularly turn to one another to identify problems, discuss and analyze them, and promote policies to solve them.

Ironically, the United States, the richest member of the OECD—which has almost tripled in national wealth in the five decades since the OECD was created—is the worst in income and wealth inequality, according to the Gini Index of 2000s (tables 2 and 3 in chapters 9 and 10). As explained earlier, the Gini coefficient is the standard statistic economists use to measure income inequality. This inequality is now rising, not just in the United States but globally. Still, it's the United States that leads the way. The levels of inequality seen today in America have no parallel anywhere in the developed world and are chiefly caused by lowering taxes on the rich combined with lower benefits for the poor, which pushes out the income gap ever wider. Thus, the OECD has come to recognize the indispensable role of the government in closing the gap by reducing inequality. Further, the organization realizes that laissez-faire economic trends toward unfettered freedom and privatization have gone too far, and it is about time for them to be reversed.

NORDIC NATIONS' RATIONALISM

The role of the government is strongly emphasized in the social democracy practiced by Nordic nations. Nordic countries have a much larger government sector and higher social expenditures, and are more regulated with a progressive tax system. All these countries spend their revenues extensively on social welfare so that the demand-side (consumption) economy can sustain a full motion, which in turn will drive the supply side. The Nordic countries tend to provide benefits to all members of society at all income levels and consequently collect a large share of revenue in taxes. The taxes and transfers have much stronger effects on the income distribution in these countries. According to a OECD report from 2014, average government tax revenues as percentage of GDP are 45 percent in this region, while they are 24 percent in the United States. And the same report indicates that the 2014 average public expenditures as a percentage of GDP were 52 percent in Sweden and 38 percent in the United States.[100] Spending as a share of GDP is a good measure of what a country spends relative to what it can afford and of the role government plays in the country's economic life.

NATIONAL EXPENDITURE CATEGORIES HIGHLIGHTED BY OECD TO PROMOTE HAPPINESS OF CITIZENS

National budgets are a way of allocating financial resources to achieve human happiness. Looking at spending as a share of the total budget provides an indication of how a country prioritizes certain allocations or functions over others.

---

100 Source: OECD Data, Latest publication, Government at a Glance, 2015.

The OECD provides a breakdown of government expenditure according to purpose, aggregating them into ten categories:

* environmental protection;
* housing and community amenities;
* recreation and culture and religion;
* defense;
* public order and safety;
* economic affairs;
* education;
* general public services;
* health; and
* social protection.

PUBLIC EXPENDITURES FOR SOCIAL PROTECTION

Social expenditures—health, education, and social protection—extended beyond those that directly promote business can reap long-term economic rewards. France is at the upper end, spending 32 percent of its government budget on social protection. Denmark spends about 30 percent, and Finland spends 31 percent. It is, however, notable that South Korea is at the other end of the scale, spending only 10 percent, with the United States just above it at 19 percent.[101]

Social protection consists of all income transfers (or benefits) in kind and in cash that a society affords to its citizen members in order to avoid or relieve poverty, or assist them in coping with a series of life contingencies or risks. All of the countries that are high spenders in the category of social protection have elected to allocate a considerably large share of their national revenue to public purposes. This reflects the mission of government and its role in society and the economy. Countries with low spending in social protection (namely, South Korea and the United States) tend more toward leaving it to the private

---

101 Ibid.

sector, with less government intervention. Spending on social protection is one way of gauging the level of government intervention in the economy—at least with respect to a commitment to ending intolerable inequities. Public spending plays a key role in the pursuit of economic growth and in ensuring that national wealth is wisely distributed to promote broad-based increases in living standards. In order to effectively achieve these objectives, the government not only must maintain fiscal balance in the long run but also effectively put the revenue it collects through taxes back into the economy via redistribution. How public expenditures contribute to economic prosperity depends on how those funds are allocated and whether they are spent efficiently.

VALIDITY OF WAGNER'S LAW

Wagner's law, also known as the law of increasing state spending—a principle named after the German economist Adolph Wagner (1835–1917)—predicts that the development of an industrial economy will be accompanied by an increased share of public expenditure in GDP because "the advent of modern industrial society will result in increasing political pressure for social progress and increased allowance for social consideration by industry." So growth in public spending is not a handicap to economic growth but an essential part of economic growth and development in all nations. We can identify a range of ways in which a rising proportion of public spending helps economies:

> Public spending has a crucial role in investment in infrastructure. There are benefits to the whole economy from having good roads, railways, electricity, and water supplies, but it is not profitable for private investors to build them. Therefore, in all countries, infrastructure investment has been driven by the public sector. Most of the recent productivity gains in the US economy were due to public investment in infrastructure, including roads and electricity during industrial boom. A recent study on health and education spending in OECD countries found that public expenditures affect GDP growth

more than private expenditures. This is consistent with the strong evidence that public spending on health care is much more efficient, in economic terms, and more effective, in terms of health objectives, than private spending on health care. Very simply, public health care is more efficient for the economy as a whole. It goes without saying that a healthy, well-educated workforce is much more productive.

* Redistribution of income increases consumer demand. This is because poorer people spend a much higher proportion of their income. So redistributing income from rich to poor through a benefits system stimulates economic growth. Thus, state-sponsored redistribution policies may accelerate the pace of a nation's economic activity by placing additional income in the hands of families with relatively high propensities to consume.

* Public services are a collective long-term insurance mechanism. It has been evidenced in industrialized economies that a public system of collective support in sickness, unemployment, old age, and so on replaces the role of the extended family in agricultural societies. With no doubt, a provision of guaranteed public services and social security motivates people to spend more instead of saving to protect themselves.

* Economists have shown that a bigger tax imposition to finance social spending does not correlate negatively with either the level or the growth of GDP per capita. There are sound reasons why countries that devote a third of their GDP to social transfers have not necessarily grown more slowly than countries that devote only a fraction of their GDP to them. There is a general benefit to social and economic stability, basically eliminating various patterns of social evils spread by no-welfare-state options—including high crime rates, depression, anxiety, stress, anger, and mistrust of government—that breed violence and destruction and in the long run lead to economic stagnation and chaos.

Social protection funds become assets to the national economy to the extent that they are well spent to bring people into the economic mainstream by covering policies that redistribute national income or provide social services for the weak and poor. It should be remembered that money collected in taxes to pay for social protection does not disappear from the economy, because the net-economic impact is positive, either as investment in human capital or funding consumption that reenters the economy. Typically, the largest social-protection programs are contributory social-insurance programs like old-age pensions or unemployment benefits. Noncontributory programs play a residual, complementary role. The US government spending of 19 percent (of GDP), is below the OECD average of 22 percent. Social protection benefits consist of cash transfers or in-kind provision of goods and services. On average across OECD countries, cash transfers are twice as large as spending on in-kind services consisting of pensions (old-age cash benefits and survivors), income support to the working age population at risk from illness or loss of earnings (disability-cash benefits, occupational injury and disease, sickness benefits, family-cash benefits, unemployment benefits, housing benefits, and other contingencies), and public health expenditure and other social services (services for the elderly and disabled people, family services, and active labor market policies). There are real economic and social benefits of public spending, but the size of spending is always the outcome of political decisions. In other words, there is no market mechanism that automatically generates larger public sectors.

VIRTUOUS QUALITY OF SOCIAL DEMOCRACY

It should be noted that the emphasis on welfare states and the development of public services were strongly associated with the rise of social-democratic governments in Europe. As long as the long-term economic advantages of higher public spending are recognized, the wisdom of the welfare state championed by social democracy should be heralded and emulated globally by all countries—if our global community is unanimously aiming at human happiness.

Neo-Keynesians and socialists often urge governments to emulate modern welfare states like Sweden. Social democracy has been the dominant political force in developing this universalistic welfare state that pervades all aspects of people's lives. It is within this system that the concept of social rights has been most fully realized because the enjoyment of benefits and services is least dependent on a person's performance in the market and is, instead, commensurate to need. Wagner's law indicates that a welfare state is an evolution from free market capitalism due to the population voting for ever-increasing social services. T. H. Marshall, a British sociologist, also identified the welfare state as a distinctive combination of democracy, welfare, and capitalism.

WELFARE STATES USHERED BY SOCIAL-DEMOCRATIC GOVERNMENTS

Examples of earlier welfare states in the modern world are Germany, all of the Nordic countries, and the Netherlands. In the period following the Second World War, many other countries in Europe moved from partial or selective provision of social services to relatively comprehensive coverage of the population. The activities of present-day welfare states extend to the provision of both cash welfare benefits (such as old-age pensions or unemployment benefits) and in-kind welfare services (such as health- or childcare services). Through these provisions, welfare states can protect the well-being and personal autonomy of their citizens, as well as influencing how their citizens consume and how they spend their time.

Social democracy has so far been the most successful socioeconomic model that affirms not only God's harmonic law but also the civic virtue Aristotle and Thomas Aquinas tried to impart to us for human happiness. Social democracy advocates a peaceful evolutionary transition of society from capitalism to socialism using established political processes. Social democracy is a political philosophy of the left or center-left that emerged in the late nineteenth century from the socialist movement in Europe, and it continues to exert influence worldwide. Its core principles agree with American liberal democrats' credo. It strongly supports a democratic welfare state, incorporating economic elements of both socialism and capitalism—thus sometimes defined as a mixed economy. This differs from traditional socialism, which aims to end the predominance of capitalism altogether.

Social democrats aim to reform capitalism democratically through government regulation and the creation of programs that work to counteract or remove the social injustice and inefficiencies they see as inherent in capitalism. As we have seen, capitalism relies too much on the growth of the economy, without balancing the distribution of this growth for sustainable long-term economic prosperity. Economic prosperity differs from economic growth measured by GDP, as economic prosperity is a policy intervention endeavor with aims of economic and social well-being of the people, whereas economic growth is simply a phenomenon of market productivity and rise in GDP. Amartya Sen, the Indian economist who was awarded the 1998 Nobel Prize in Economics for his contributions to welfare economics and social choice theory, points out that economic growth (GDP) is only one aspect of the process of economic development (prosperity). Economic prosperity typically involves improvements in a variety of indicators—such as literacy rates, life expectancy, and poverty rates—which are more related to human happiness.

Essentially, a country's economic prosperity is to promote human happiness through the common good, which encompasses health, education, and welfare, among other things. Nonetheless, these factors are closely related to economic growth, in which economic growth is feeding the society by redistribution, and societal welfare, which in turn helps drive the growth. Therefore, social democrats are often called "reformists" in favor of change through gradual reforms in the capitalistic system. Social-democratic parties are among the largest parties in most countries in Europe, and there are strong indications that globally more people share the basic ideals of social democrats than any other political ideology. There are 115 countries, including Canada and all the advanced nations of Europe, that are direct members of Socialist International (SI) today—except the United States. SI calls on all men and women committed to peace and progress to work together in order to translate the dream into reality—that is, happiness for all human beings on the planet.

Modern social democrats are in favor of a capitalist market economy but with a strong government intervention, advocating for a progressive income tax, publicly funded health care, and free or almost-free university education. Let's keep in mind that they do not object to the concept of privatized industry and services. Instead, they advocate for public-private partnerships to deliver social services. There are three basic characteristics in social democracy—responsibility, regulation, and redistribution—reflecting the fact that the European social-democratic model is more than just a social model in the narrow sense. On the one hand, it influences social relationships, cultural institutions and behavior, learning, and diffusion of knowledge. On the other hand, it influences production, employment, and productivity, and thus, consequent growth, competitiveness, and all the other objectives a capitalistic economy cherishes.

Social democracy is not simply a political or social model, but it's an inclusive socio-economic-political model that embraces everything in human community to support and sustain human happiness through common actions. In this respect, the Nordic model is the most comprehensive system, with a high degree of emphasis on redistribution and social benefits financed by taxes.

Chapter 14

ACTIVE PEACE
THROUGH HUMANISM

The definition of peace has been loosely understood throughout history. In the political sense, it has been perceived as the absence of war or conflict. In a given society, it has been viewed as the absence of discordance. On an individual level, traditionally peace has been understood as the passive, simplistic state of tranquility, or freedom from disturbance. But the real "peace" to me is an *active peace*, or what Norwegian sociologist Johan Galtung calls: "positive peace—integration of human society." I would like to broaden his idea of positive peace by conceptualizing an active peace that contains a perpetual motion of humanism. Active peace calls for civic virtue by which everyone benefits, with no winners and losers.

HUMANISM IS THE BEDROCK FOR ACTIVE PEACE

Humanism is a mental attitude, philosophy, and life stance centered on human interests and values, stressing an individual's worth and capacity for self-realization through intellect and rational thinking. Humanism is, of course, not a newly developed idea. It goes back to ancient Greece and later Rome.

It is no coincidence that many of our legal codes go back to Rome and many scientific and technical terms and ideas back to ancient Greece. In particular, Greece has profoundly influenced modern philosophy, religion, and science. We frequently use the term "Renaissance humanism" to refer to the intellectual, literary, and scientific movement of the fourteenth to sixteenth centuries, a movement that revived every branch of cultural learning from early Greco-Roman antiquity. The humanist thinkers of this early period include Plato, Aristotle, and Cicero, to name a few. But as outlined in the beginning of the book, the value of modern humanism is derived not only from early Greco-Roman humanism but also from the Christian tradition. The word *humanitas* was used by Cicero (106–43 BC), a Roman philosopher, politician, and orator, to describe the formation of an ideal orator. Cicero emphasized that ideal orator should be cultivated and educated to possess aggregate virtues suitable for an active life of public service. Cicero examined the qualities of what he perceived to be the ideal orator, determining that character is essential to make "rhetoric" the science of speaking well. For this, the ideal orator must possess all the virtues of the orator, since no one can speak well without being equipped with morally good character. As an effective means of moving leaders or fellow citizens toward one political course or another, eloquence was akin to a power engine.

Consequently, humanists cultivated rhetoric as the medium through which all other virtues could be communicated and fulfilled. Of course, Cicero himself, a member of the Roman Senate, was the most influential practitioner and theorist of ancient rhetoric who ever lived. Humanitas means the development of human virtue—the excellence of humankind—in all its forms, to its fullest extent. A style of thought rather than a formal doctrine, humanitas postulates the importance of humans as cultivated beings with full control of the moral universe. The term thus implies not only such qualities associated with the modern word "humanity"—understanding, benevolence, compassion, and mercy—but also more characteristics such as fortitude, judgment, prudence, eloquence, and honor. Hence, the possessor of humanitas could not be merely a sedentary and isolated philosopher but an active participant in public life, with a fine balance of action and contemplation. Such fulfilled qualities, undoubtedly required by policy makers in government, would highlight civic virtue.

For Renaissance humanists, there was nothing outdated or outworn about the writings of Plato, Cicero, or Aristotle. Compared with the typical doctrines of medieval Christianity, these philosophical ideals had a fresh, radical, almost avant-garde tonality. Classical virtue, in the examples of which the literature abounded, was not an abstract idea but a quality that could be tested in the real world. They trusted the scientific method, evidence, and reason to discover truths about the universe and placed human welfare and happiness at the center of their ethical decision making. The emphasis on virtuous action as the goal of learning was a founding principle of humanism and continued to exert a strong influence throughout the course of modern civilization.

FRANCESCO PETRARCA AS FATHER OF HUMANISM

Francesco Petrarca (1304–74), known in English as Petrarch, was an Italian scholar and poet and one of the early nonreligious humanists. He is often called the "father of humanism," as he was not only the first to revive antique knowledge as wisdom but also the first to deplore a transcendental concept of life, contrasting to a mundane, human, and naturalistic view that focused on nature and humankind. But, Petrarca, devout Christian yet, unashamedly wrote secular works about love, passion, and the unending quest to understand the human soul. This new spirit broke away from theology and the Church, and scientific inquiry gained ground with humanism.

After Petrarch, humanism spread first through Italy and then into other parts of Europe. During the mid- to late-fourteenth century, a number of scholars in Florence followed Petrarch's lead and collected and studied ancient works. These scholars lectured about ancient literature and imitated the style of the ancient works, and eventually the city of Florence became a center of humanistic learning. The Italian humanists, of course, identified strongly with Rome. The northern Europeans, however, did not have such a strong tie to Rome, yet wholeheartedly embraced Christianity, with compassion for fellow men and humility to God. Although humanism in northern Europe and England sprang largely from Italian sources, it did not emerge exclusively as an outgrowth of later Italian humanism. The humanists of the northern Renaissance placed a greater emphasis on Christianity, education, and reform. They sought to combine the best of the ancient Greek and Roman world with the best that Christianity had to offer. The most famous of the northern or Christian humanists was Erasmus of Rotterdam (1466–1536). Erasmus had an interest in education and religious reform. He believed that people should study the ancient classics and the Bible in an effort to reform themselves and society.

CHRISTIAN HUMANISM OF NORTHERN EUROPE

Christian humanism is centered on the belief that human freedom, individual conscience, and unencumbered rational inquiry are compatible with the practice of Christianity or even intrinsic in its doctrine. It represents a philosophical union of Christian faith and classical humanist principles. The ancient roots of Christian humanism have been seen in Jesus's teachings and Saint Paul's emphasis on freedom from the external constraints of religious law, as well as the appeal to classical learning by the Christian apologists. Although its roots reach back to antiquity, Christian humanism grew more directly out of Christian scholasticism and Renaissance humanism, both of which developed from the rediscovery in Europe of classical Latin and Greek texts. For this reason, sometimes northern humanism is identified with Christian humanism. Christian humanism attempted to use the scholarly techniques of intellect and apply them to the study of the Bible, ignoring prior medieval interpretations. Nonetheless, the quest for happiness, the good life, is still the central task of these humanists. They believe a person is capable and responsible for the realization of his or her dreams, but more than that, he or she has a duty to his or her fellow beings to fulfill the common good because that is the only way to create happiness.

Northern European humanists also developed the doctrine that the people's duty is to promote human welfare through intellect, morality, and justice, believing that the highest good is to perfect human happiness and civilization. They recognized that a noble humanism requires faith in something larger than human intellect. They agreed with Plato, who believed that the physical world around us is not real; rather, it is constantly changing, and thus one can never say what it really is. But an invisible world of unchanging and absolute truth exists. A number of proofs of this ideal world can be found. In geometry, for example, a perfect circle—a line equidistant from a center point—does not exist in the physical world. All physical circles, such as wheels, drawings, and so on, are not perfectly round. Yet our mind can conceive of a perfect circle. Since this concept could not come from the physical world, it must come from an ideal world. Another proof concerns moral perfection. We can conceive of a morally perfect person, even though the people we know around us are not morally perfect. So where does someone get this idea of moral perfection? Since it could not have been obtained from the world around us, it must have come from an ideal world. This ideal world is known to us today as God. Enveloping all that is real, God—and therefore everything He is (eternal, omniscient, etc.)—is justifiably real. Everything else is just mortal imperfection. Aristotle, a disciple of Plato, describes human intellect as coming from without, from an eternal and omnipresent thinker, although he did not call it God.

The acknowledgment of an eternal being in classical humanism was later recognized as deism, which became the complementing components of Western civilization. Religions in this context facilitate the participation of human intellect in the higher consciousness that emanates the true virtuous spirit capable of taming barbarism into humane culture—or civilization. The secular humanists who claim that human beings are fully capable of satisfying themselves without the assistance of God or transcendent reality still do not deny that human intellect can potentially be expanded. Those secular humanists, however, do not proclaim that we obtain perfect knowledge by reaching out for the divine wisdom of God. Aristotle considered perfect knowledge as the highest virtue. In my opinion, this virtue is not moral obligation in itself but the beauty of knowledge that shines from the wisdom of God to benefit all who can bask in its light. A virtuous human recognizes that all human beings are dependent on one another's help. This compels him or her to exercise compassion in every relation with people around him or her and the world. This is what Christ's teaching is all about—humanistic concern and care.

Based on human intellect, Western humanism postulates human greatness, freedom, and character formation through learning Greco-Roman thoughts, later poured into Christianity, which highlights a spiritual relation to the world through participation in the divine logos. Owing largely to the influence of Plato and Aristotle, Western philosophy became the spiritual guide for governments, emphasizing a practical discipline in the quest for human happiness and civil society. In this quest, modern humanists believe in democracy, open government, and human rights and support action on world poverty and the environment. Modern humanists have renewed the question, echoing the basic quest of Greek classical humanists: "What is the good life, and how can it be attained in this world?"

ACTIVE HUMANISM OF MODERN WORLD

Burgeoning humanist organizations exist worldwide today, varying their concerns and activities according to the situation at hand. They are also vigilant to the fact that there is a faction within the circle of humanists that promotes individualism, which triggers the expansion of capitalism by asserting that the rights of private property take precedence over the rights of the community as a whole. True humanists, however (mostly Christian), are recognizing that an acquisitive and profit-motivated society (heavily adhering to capitalism) has shown itself to be grossly defective and that a change must be brought in to mend the flaw. A socialized and cooperative economic order must be established with equitable distribution of the means of life, because all citizens in a civil society equally deserve well-being and happiness. The goal of humanism is a free and equitable society in which people voluntarily and intelligently cooperate for the common good.

Undoubtedly, good humanists would agree that every person is entitled, as a matter of right, to basic goods: housing, food, clothes, health care, education, and protection against victimization and crime, especially for children, the elderly, and those with mental or physical disabilities. These rights have nothing to do with anyone's personal character, background, or attitude. For example, drunks and other addicts, the incurably lazy, and those considered immoral or otherwise obnoxious are still entitled to the same basic minimum to maintain human dignity. All social primary goods—liberty and opportunity, income and wealth, and the bases of self-respect—are to be distributed equitably. These general principles of humanism, derived logically and rationally, can establish agreed-upon standards for civil society through government policies whose sole aim is to protect and promote such humanism. The role of the government is to encourage citizens to perpetuate humanism through which individual and collective peace can be guaranteed for society.

SOCIALIST INTERNATIONAL (SI) AND HUMANISM

Contemporary social democracy, embedded in humanism, is a political movement that seeks to reform capitalism to align it with the ethical ideals of social justice and ultimately to create peaceful civil societies. Contemporary social democratic policies include support for a welfare state, Keynesian macroeconomic policies, and collective bargaining arrangements to balance the power of capital and labor. Examples include the Nordic model and the social market-economy model used by West Germany after World War II. Social democratic political parties around the world, such as the British Labor Party, the Socialist Party of France, and the Social Democratic Party of Germany, are joined in an international federation called Socialist International (SI), which advocates for the creation of legal reforms and economic-redistribution programs to eliminate economic class disparities between the rich and the poor. SI, whose origins go back to the early international organizations of the labor movement, has existed in its present form since 1951, when it was reestablished at the Frankfurt Congress. Since then it has been increasingly active and has grown considerably in membership, more than doubling the number of its members in recent years.

Labor, social democratic, and socialist parties are now a major political force in many countries around the world, with numerous member parties of SI leading governments or representing the main opposition force against capitalism. Over sixty member parties in over fifty-five different countries and territories are currently in the SI coalition. Notably, most promote practical social democratic policies, including the promotion of a welfare state and the creation of an economic democracy as a means to secure workers' rights. For example, the Nordic model relies on institutions working closely together with the government. The trade unions, for example, are strongly involved in the administration of unemployment insurance and training, and the model establishes an effective labor-market policy that results in high employment rates. Contrastingly, the US trade union density has historically been very low, falling from 22 percent in 1980 to 11.4 percent in 2010,[102] while in the Scandinavian countries the collective agreements through trade unions cover 82 percent of employees, and the trend is still rising. Strong unions would have helped to reduce inequality. As witnessed, the weaker unions of America have made it easier for corporate employers to hire and fire workers since there are no binding contracts with any unions that they have to abide by.

In terms of institutional structure and policies, the strategies of the most successful European countries (Denmark, Finland, and Sweden, which all fall under the Scandinavian model) differ greatly from the US system, particularly in terms of welfare and government involvement, as well as in their commitments to economic redistribution and employment training. In contrast to the United States, these European nations rely on proactive industrial policies, with the government supporting information technology and agencies

---

102 *Union Members Summary Bureau of Labor Statistics,* January 27, 2012, "Union membership in the private sector has fallen under 7 percent—levels not seen since 1932. The decline in unionization since the Second World War in the United States has resulted in a pronounced rise in income and wealth inequality with disappearance of middle class income class," retrieved February 26, 2012.

promoting research for local clusters. These Scandinavian countries are at the very top on the Global Peace Index (see figure 14, chapter 11), while the national peacefulness of the United States is heading backward to the level of underdeveloped nations. Remember that the architecture of peaceful societies is engineered by humanists and noble characters whose aims are compassionately linked to human happiness.

The more humanists are abundant in the world, the more it will approximate the characteristics of the ideal world—the actualization of harmony and beauty. As Christ taught human beings to pray to God, "Thy kingdom come, thy will be done on earth as in heaven," a good life on Earth is possible only through humanism aligning our conscience and intellect with God's wisdom. By humbling our soul to God's wisdom, we can generate virtuous energy and perpetuate active peace to sustain human happiness—the good life. Active peace, or the collective peaceful minds of citizens free from anxiety, fear, and all other negative emotions that breed social evils, can ensure societal prosperity—an earthly kingdom. The opposite side of such active peace is the state of increasing economic inequality and social injustice, leading citizens into depression, anxiety, stress, anger, and mistrust in government, which spreads violence and discordance in society and ultimately destroys human civilization.

Humanism is none other than God's wisdom absorbed by active human souls utilizing the universal intellect to generate peace and harmony on Earth. Virtue, then, is a visible manifestation of virtuous souls that shine the wisdom of God to benefit all. As everything in the universe is held together by harmonic law, a civil society is held together by humanism, which brings forth human virtue obeying the same law. Such sacred bonding is demonstrated by Φ, whose purpose is to maintain harmony in the cosmos to which Earth planet belongs. At the same time, all things in the cosmic sphere are bonded by mathematical π—the infinite love of God. The harmonic law is undeniably creating universal beauty in everything we perceive through tangible or intangible form, whether it is human behavior or nature's course of propagation, exuded from the divine spirit. Thus, the golden ratio (Φ) applies not only to the motion of the universe but also to human behavior to create beauty on Earth.

History has shown that when civic virtue is neglected—when enjoying individual life becomes more important than preserving values such as compassion, humility, temperance, fairness, and moral integrity, and when those in economic power think that they can tweak the moral value and defraud the weak to protect their wealth and that self-interest is more important than the joint prosperity of all citizens, when all that happens—harmonic law is violated, and consequently the blossom of any given civilization will start to wilt and decay. When this harmonic law is violated, the fabric of a civil society begins to crumble, and civilization will eventually be destroyed. Taking the necessary steps to turn matters around and prevent these scenarios from developing is the duty of governments. Only humanistic government actions, observing the divine proportion of harmonic law, can reverse the course to bring back the equilibrium of civil society and maintain the dynamics of active peace desired by all citizens.

CONCLUSION

The coexistence of modern capitalism and democracy can be traced back to the modern welfare state created in the postwar period, which enabled a relatively stable political atmosphere and widespread support for capitalism. This period of history is often referred to as the "golden age of capitalism" with democratic capitalism, which is an ideology that involves the combination of a democratic political system with a capitalist economic system. This ideology supports a capitalist economy subject to control by the democratic political system. As the Western world has passionately guarded democracy for human rights and freedom, that freedom eventually spread its wings toward excess and greed, unchecked by proper government regulations. This resulted in the creation of enormous inequality of income/wealth and economic anarchy in the capitalistic society of today. We must understand, however, that inequality, the real source of the evil, is not the inevitable side effect of capitalism—if government policy positively works to reduce inequality by addressing equitableness.

Let's not forget that the production of these large corporations is mainly for profit, not for necessity demanded by consumers. The result of these developments is an oligarchy of private capital generating enormous power that cannot be effectively checked, even by a democratically organized political society. The economic system, particularly in America today, is run by big business and revolves around money and capital assets tilted toward pure capitalism—an economic system with little governmental interference. The situation is exacerbated by the fact that the members of legislative bodies selected by political parties are covertly financed or otherwise influenced by private capitalists who, for their selfish purposes, can manipulate the legislature. The consequence is then that the representatives of the people do not sufficiently protect the interests of the underprivileged sections of the population as discussed extensively in chapter 5 and 6 of this book.

Moreover, under existing conditions, directly or indirectly, private capitalists inevitably control the main sources of information—mass media. Mass media in capitalist societies therefore has become both the crony of a capitalistic system and a means of reinforcing it. Indeed, in the case of the current mass media, which is privately owned and controlled, its overwhelming concern is also for profit.

Technological progress, discarding human labor, frequently results in more unemployment rather than in an easing of the burden of work for all. Workers are constantly in fear of losing their jobs, and there is no provision that all those able and willing workers will always find adequate employment, since production is requiring less and less human capital. It is fair to say then that the profit motive, with along competition among capitalists, is responsible for instability in the labor market and employment as technology improvements replace human labor. Unhindered competition leads to an aggressive application of technology in order to reduce human-labor costs, while workers have become more conscious than ever of their dependence upon a capitalistic society. It does not mean that this dependence is a manifestation of organic ties as a constructive force, but it is rather seen as a way to protect workers' economic survival and natural rights. Within such misplaced social mores, contemporary humanity is freely expressed by the egotistical drives of capitalists and workers, spurred both by aggressive profit and defensive survival motives, resulting in human value deterioration. Thus, all human beings, whatever their position in society may be, are suffering from this progressive deterioration of human values amid twisted social consciousness. Being prisoners of their own egotism, men and women feel insecure and deprived of the simple enjoyment of life, losing their humane connectedness to society.

Enlightenment thinkers would agree that the crucial element that has been missing from the contemporary democratic idea is its fundamental character—humanism. Humanism is the extension of participatory democracy and an expansion of global consciousness, emphasizing the welfare of humankind and building a more humane society through healthy social norms based on sound rationality and a solid understanding of universal law. Humanism is a philosophy of compassion while in tune with the science of today. It stresses human rationality and responsibility to lead meaningful, ethical lives, adding to the greater good of humanity, both individually and collectively. A society shaped by moral principles and democratic ethos has a moral obligation to its citizens, which highlights governmental actions, where necessary, to assure opportunity, meet basic human needs, and provide justice in economic life to all citizens. Thus, the rational choices of governing institutions must be judged by how they protect or undermine the life and dignity of humankind and the common good of society, recognizing that decisions on investment, trade, aid, and technological development should protect human life and promote human rights, especially for those most in need, wherever they might live on our planet.

The motions of all matters in the universe yield to an uncanny balance supported by the universal law of harmony established by the Prime Mover (God). Our man-made human society is no exception, being a part of this large cosmic nature, in obeying the same universal law to survive and flourish. The law of harmony, the splendor of the universe, is clearly demonstrated in the mathematical symbol Φ, called the golden ratio, divine proportion, or golden mean. This ratio is ubiquitously applied to observable nature on Earth, shining the beauty of harmony, and likewise it sets the moral tone in human behaviors in the society, pointing out that the greedy behaviors of humans are in violation of this omnipotent law. Such violation of universal law can eventually ignite the flame of destruction not only within human civilization but also on planet Earth if not abated to maintain the delicate balance of the nature of Earth. When this preset balance is interrupted by human greed and ignorance, our human race will eventually face an inevitable doom. Thus, capitalism and democracy, the ends and means, must be in harmony with each other if we desire a peaceful civilization on Earth.

So far, with the latest scientific knowledge of the universe, there is no other good planet in sight that we can migrate to. That is, Earth is the only planet that has the perfect arrangement in balance for us to survive and thrive. Earth space does not expand; thus we have to live with limited space and resources conjointly. That is to say, we have a communal and global moral obligation to avoid the disastrous consequences of disharmony in human society facing explosive global population growth. Humankind has evolved on Earth over a long period of time, from single cell bacteria eons ago to become what we are today by symbiotic evolution.

In view of the historical context of human evolution and witnessing the perilous side effects of capitalism, I am truly convinced the grave evils of inequality must be subdued by establishment of prudent public policy based on welfare economics adopted by Nordic nations (Denmark, Finland, Norway, Iceland and Sweden) that would aim at the happiness of all citizens of society. In such an economy, government's role is vital to enforce a progressive income tax system that expects mega-rich people pay greater amount in taxes in much higher tax rate than a low income earners. The objective is of course to transfer income from those who are mega-rich to those who suffer poverty. The governmental action of redistribution of income and wealth ultimately is to maintain harmony in human societies upholding the sanctity that every human being is not only equally created but also equally deserves happiness (well-being).

BIBLIOGRAPHY

Adams, John. "*Essay of 'Thoughts on Government*: Applicable to the Present State of the American Colonies,'" 1766, p. 306. Extracted from *The Revolutionary Writings of John Adams*. Indianapolis, IN: Liberty Fund, 2000. (See footnote 50, page 129, of this book for annotation.)

Aristotle. *Nicomachean Ethics*. Translated by David Ross. New York: Oxford University Press, 2009; and *Politics*.Ttranslated by Carnes Lord. Chicago: University of Chicago 2013. Aristotle provides a thorough examination of human activities that brings happiness, well lived life. Aristotle emphasizes in his book, Nicomachean Ethics, human happiness that consists in activity of the soul according to rationality. Hence the rational part of the soul can be considered a person's identity. In practical terms, this activity of soul is expressed through virtue. What Aristotle wants to say in *Politics* is that the objective of the state is to make the life of the individual noble and happy by looking after the security and general welfare of its citizens. Undoubtedly this is the most important function of the state. In other words, the state is the supreme organization to look after the interests of all citizens in a balanced way. After all *"the political association which we call a state exists not simply for the purpose of living together, but for the sake of noble actions"* as he stated.

Beschloss, Michael, and Hugh Sidey. *The Presidents of the United States of America*. Washington, DC: White House Historical Association, Copyright 2006.

Catholic Encyclopedia. New York: Robert Appleton Company. http://www.newadvent.org/cathen/07543b.htm. Last visit 10/26/16

Buddha, *Dhammacakkappavattana Sutta: Setting in Motion the Wheel of Truth* is a Buddhist text, memorized by the Buddha's disciples and passed down in an oral lineage and a few centuries later they were written down, retaining much of the convention of the oral tradition. Translated and "Introduction" by Soma Thera. Kandy, Sri Lanka: Buddhist Publication Society, 2010.

Ferguson, Adam. *An Essay on the History of* Civil Society. Online Library of Liberty, 2016. http://oll.libertyfund.org/titles/ferguson-an-essay-on-the-history-of-civil-society.

Jefferson, Thomas. *Declaration of Independence.* Marietta, GA: Discovery Enterprises, 1970. (Note: Drafted originally by Thomas Jefferson, although coauthored with other founders). Thomas Jefferson is the most legendary president of America and his legacy still shines as bright as the North Star in the heavens. The American myth is created by his immortal words in the Declaration for Independence. Although the Declaration of Independence, adopted on July 4, 1776, has undergone a series of revisions from Jefferson's original draft, his words remain essentially unchanged, stated as "*We hold these truths to be self-evident, that all men are created equal, that they are endowed by their Creator with certain unalienable Rights; that among these are Life, Liberty, and the pursuit of Happiness.*"

Kant, Immanuel. *Critique of Pure Reason.* The Cambridge Edition of the Works of Immanual Kant. Translated by Paul Guyer and Allen Wood. Cambridge University Press, 1998.

Kepler, Johannes. *Harmonices Mundi* (Harmony of the World). Translated by E. J. Aiton, Alistair Matheson Duncan, and Judith Veronica Field. American Philosophical Society, 1997.

Locke, John. *Two Treatises on Government (1680–1690).* Edited by Peter Laslett. Cambridge University Press, 1970.

O'Sullivan, John. "The Great Nation of Futurity," *The United States Democratic Review* 6, no. 23 (1839): 426–30.